size of cans	weight	approximate cup measure
no. ½	7¾ to 8½ oz.	1 cup
no. 300	13½ fl. oz.	1¾ cups
no. 1	1 lb.	2 cups
no. 303	1 lb. or 15 fl. oz.	2 cups
no. 2	1 lb. 4 oz.	2 ½ cups
no. 2½	1 lb. 13 oz.	3½ cups

weights and measures

pinch or dash	less than ⅛ teaspoon
1 teaspoon	⅓ tablespoon
3 teaspoons	1 tablespoon
2 tablespoons	⅛ cup
4 tablespoons	¼ cup
5 tablespoons plus 1 teaspoon	⅓ cup
10 tablespoons plus 2 teaspoons	⅔ cup
12 tablespoons	¾ cup
16 tablespoons	1 cup
2 cups	1 pint
2 pints	1 quart
4 quarts	1 gallon
8 quarts	1 peck
4 pecks	1 bushel
16 ounces	1 pound
1 fluid ounce	2 tablespoons

The COPCO
POTS and PANS
COOKBOOK

The COPCO POTS and PANS COOKBOOK

Ann Seranne and Joan Wilson

Copco thanks Ann Seranne and Joan Wilson for finding our porcelainized cast iron utensils to be exceptionally fine quality cookware for their excellent and varied recipes.

Also published as The POTS and PANS COOKBOOK

Doubleday & Company, Inc., Garden City, New York

PREFACE

This is a book to read first, then to cook from first chapter to last. It is a cookbook for the novice as well as for the experienced homemaker.

If you are a beginner cook, I hope it will inspire you to consider carefully your kitchen cookware before you buy it. Don't be sold a slew of bright, shiny pots and pans by a handsome, fast-talking door-to-door salesman, like one young girl I know. Buy the best quality heavy-duty cookware you can find to cook in that is handsome enough to also serve from at table. Buy just one or two pieces at a time, for good cookware is expensive, and buy only what you really need. You'll be amazed at how many complete dinners you'll be able to turn out with one or two skillets and a saucepan. Go on from there, adding another piece of matching cookware as you need it and can afford it. If you begin at the beginning and "cook along" with this book, and I don't mean every recipe, but those that appeal to you from each chapter, you'll be an excellent cook before you finish it, and what's more you'll enjoy it. You'll find that cooking is easier and more fun when you have the right kind of equipment.

If you are an experienced homemaker, with lots of cooking years behind you, I hope this book will give you pause for thought and incentive to evaluate the pots and pans and miscellany that you have acquired throughout your cooking years. If you would throw out or give away those tricky gadgets, cunning saucepans, and quaint accessories that are cluttering your kitchen drawers and cupboards and start all over again, you'd find that preparing daily meals takes on new life. You'll save, of course, those good, heavy-bottomed pots and black iron skillets in which you cook some favorite dishes, but you'll add some new colorful cookware which will give both your cooking and your kitchen a much-needed face lifting.

Your kitchen cookware is as important to fine cooking as any ingredient that goes into the dish—perhaps more important—for the wrong pot can spoil good food as surely as a rotten egg or rancid butter.

Don't be a compulsive buyer.

Don't buy indiscriminately.

Buy good utensils. Buy the best you can find. Take care of them and they will last you a lifetime.

Every recipe in this book has been carefully tested to make it the best possible. Your new culinary wardrobe makes the recipes really work.

Ann Seranne
For the authors

CONTENTS

The COPCO
POTS and PANS
COOKBOOK

EQUIPPING THE KITCHEN

The proper equipment is necessary for efficient cooking. It need not be much to start with, for you can do wonders with little, but whether it is a two-tined fork or a seven-quart casserole it should be the best quality that money can buy.

To be a good cook you need three things: good raw ingredients, the desire to cook them carefully, and quality equipment.

Importance of Good Cookware

After your stove and refrigerator, your cookware is first in importance. Certainly you need a wooden spoon, a spatula, some mixing bowls, measuring cups, and so on, but these utensils are incidental in cost compared to your cookware, which is a major investment. You can open many cans with a can opener, but you don't come up with much of a dish without a pot to cook the ingredients in. And that pot should be a good one for maximum flavor, for eye appeal, and for economy.

There is a right pot or pan for each recipe and for each method of food preparation. For instance, liquid in a tall pot takes twice as long to reach a boil as that in a low pot of larger diameter. If food must be covered with liquid while cooking, it takes a great deal more liquid to cover the food in a tall container than in one with ample diameter to accommodate the food in one or two layers. You need a specific size casserole for one recipe; another size for another recipe. You need a proper saucepan for a smooth sauce, a flameproof, ovenproof container with a tight-fitting cover for the slow simmering of stews and for braising foods. You need heavy pans that will not tip over and will hold a constant internal temperature so that liquids can be kept at barely a simmer without constant adjustment of the heat beneath it or around it. You need skillets that conduct heat evenly over the entire cooking surface so that foods brown evenly without burning.

Before buying, think of style as well as purpose. Your basic cookware can be not only utilitarian, but decorative in your kitchen and can do double duty as both cooking utensils and serving dishes.

Today, houseware departments in stores gleam with a bewildering array of many types and models of cookware to choose form. Ceramic, glass, copper, aluminum, stainless steel, and pottery are all available, but the best are heavy enamel- or porcelain-covered cast iron. The slick surface does not discolor foods and is easy to clean. The slow, even heat which can be maintained in cast iron makes this type of cookware perfection. It is made in a wide selection of decorator's colors to fit the color scheme of any home. It will remain attractive for years and give the maximum of efficiency so that, in the long run, it costs less than cookware of lesser quality. Add to this the amount of food you are apt to burn or spoil in lightweight pots and pans, and you'll pay for your fine, colorful cookware in no time at all.

After selecting the minimum basic cookware, which will depend to some extent on the type of dishes that appeal to you and the number you are cooking for, you can add systematically a few new pieces or one new pot once a month or once every six months, depending on your cooking needs and your pocketbook.

You do not need different equipment for top of the stove cooking and for oven cooking. Most cookware is designed for both uses. Skillets are being made with metal handles and tight-fitting covers so they can do yeoman service both over direct heat and in the oven. Casseroles are interchangeable with saucepans, Dutch ovens, cocottes or stock pots, depending on their size. It should not be necessary to remind you to use potholders when removing a dish from the oven whether it is a metal-handled skillet or a casserole.

For years homemakers have been adjusting recipes to suit a particular utensil. Now it's time to reverse this procedure. So before buying any one piece of cookware, plan first the dishes you are going to cook in it and how many people you are going to cook for. "What can I cook in it?" should be your first question. And second, "Do I really need it?"

Cookware for the Complete Kitchen

	Liquid Capacity
10-inch skillet with tight-fitting cover	1½ quarts
12-inch skillet with tight-fitting cover	2½ quarts
1½-quart covered saucepan	
2-quart covered saucepan	
3-quart covered saucepan	
Small open baker (10×6×2)	1½ quarts
Large open baker (14×8½×2)	3 quarts
14-inch diameter or rectangular roasting pan	3½ quarts
Individual au gratin dishes	1½ to 2 cups
11- or 12-inch chicken fryer with high tight-fitting cover	4 quarts
1½-quart covered casserole	
2½- or 3-quart covered casserole	
5- or 5½-quart covered casserole	
7- or 8-quart covered casserole	
Loaf pan (8½×4½×2¾)	1½ quarts

Kitchen Cutlery

One of the most important kitchen tools is the knife, and two really good ones are better than a dozen of poor quality. The best are made of plain, rustable carbon steel. These will take on a razor sharp edge much more easily than knives made of the harder stainless steel. Then you need a real butcher's steel on which to sharpen them.

If you need a lesson in sharpening a knife, ask your butcher to show you how. Wash knives as soon as you have finished using them and don't drop them carelessly into a sink of sudsy water where they can give you a nasty cut. Remove any tarnish on the blades with steel wool. A magnetic wall holder is the best way to keep knives safe and in good condition.

The Two Most Important Kitchen Knives

A paring knife with a 4½-inch angled blade that tapers to a sharp point for peeling, slicing, and trimming

A heavy chef's knife with an angled blade about 8 inches long tapering to a sharp point for halving, slicing, dicing, and chopping

Additional Kitchen Knives Nice to Have

A carving knife with a 9-inch blade for carving roasts and poultry

A boning knife for cutting through joints and removing bones from meat

A serrated-edge knife for slicing baked goods and bread

Table Ware

In addition to your basic and most essential cookware, which will double as attractive serving dishes, you will need some china, silver, and glass. Place settings for six would be a good beginning. Then you will want to have a salad bowl with servers, a salt and pepper mill, a table carving set and some baskets for serving hot biscuits and breads.

Kitchen Utensils

Again start with the few basic utensils that are absolutely necessary for cooking the simplest dish. Add extra utensils as you need them and as you gain cooking experience.

Basic and Necessary Kitchen Utensils

An assortment of wooden spoons
A small wooden chopping board or bread board
A swivel-bladed knife for peeling fruits and vegetables
A pastry brush for spreading melted butter or barbecue
    sauce over meats and chickens
A pair of kitchen tongs for turning chicken and chops
Several rubber spatulas; the slim bottle-scraper kind
    are best
A kitchen pepper mill
A can opener
A bottle opener
A sieve for straining liquids and sifting flour
A colander for draining vegetables and spaghetti or
    noodles
A 4-sided grater for grating hard cheese and shredding
    soft cheese and vegetables
A set of mixing bowls
A long-handled two-tined fork
A slotted spoon
A pancake turner
A flexible steel spatula
A tea kettle
A coffee maker (tea pot, too, if you like tea)
A good rotary or electric beater
A set of dry measuring cups (¼, ⅓, ½ and 1 cup)

A liquid measuring cup or cups (1 cup, 1 pint, 1 quart)
A set of measuring spoons (¼ teaspoon, ½ teaspoon, 1 teaspoon and 1 tablespoon)
A small wire cake rack
String
Cheesecloth
A juice extractor
A bulb meat baster
A potato masher
Kitchen scissors
A baking sheet or jelly roll pan
A rolling pin
A pastry board, cloth and rolling pin cover
A large needle and heavy thread
Refrigerator and freezer containers
Roll of transparent film
Roll each of lightweight and heavy-duty aluminum foil
Roll of wax paper
Roll of paper towels
Pot holders and kitchen towels

Additional Kitchen Utensils, Nice to Have

A small and a large wire whisk
A food mill or an electric blender
A grooved wooden carving board
An egg slicer
A soup and sauce ladle
A lime or lemon squeezer
A meat grinder
A meat thermometer
A candy thermometer

A melon ball scoop
An electric mixer
Pastry bags and a variety of tubes
Poultry shears
Poultry skewers
A mortar and pestle
A wire salad basket
An 8-inch square cake pan
Two 8- or 9-inch layer cake pans
A 9-inch pie plate
A toaster
A sandwich and waffle maker
A pancake griddle
A spice rack
A popover or muffin pan
A 6-inch skillet for small pancakes and crepes
An 8-inch omelet pan with non-stick coating
A fondue set

How to Use Recipes in This Book

1. Take the necessary time to be accurate.
2. Read recipe through, and assemble all ingredients and utensils.
3. Measure carefully:

   Use glass measuring cups with graduated markings and lip for easy pouring for liquids.

   Use nested unit measuring cups and standard measuring spoons for dry ingredients and shortening. Fill to top and level off with straight-edged knife.

4. Use the cookware specified in each recipe.

1

WHAT YOU CAN COOK
IN TWO SKILLETS

Perhaps the most important kitchen cookware for any cook are skillets with tight-fitting covers. This is a good place to start if you are just beginning to equip your kitchen or decide to turn over a new pots-and-pans-leaf, for skillets are more important than saucepans. You can use them in innumerable ways in addition to their original function of sautéing or pan frying meat, fish, poultry or eggs. You can make sauces in a skillet, cook vegetables and rice, heat soups or stews, poach fruits in syrup and so on, but you can't very well sauté hamburgers or fry eggs in a saucepan.

At least two skillets are essential for any kitchen. Select one that is 10 inches in diameter and a larger one that is 12 inches in diameter. It is important that these are made of heavy thick-gauge metal that conducts heat evenly so that foods brown evenly without burning. The close-fitting covers make it possible to braise or stew meat, fish or chicken in them after they have been gently browned, and the liquid may be kept at a gentle simmer without rapid loss of moisture and flavor.

If you select skillets with metal handles they can also go in the oven and this further extends their many uses, and if you select handsome skillets that fit in with your color scheme, they will not only make bright additions to your kitchen, but may be used as serving dishes as well.

With two handsome skillets you can prepare and serve many meals, with only two pans to wash, and the new scratch-resistant, non-stick coating prevents food from sticking and makes skillets a joy to clean. A wipe with a soapy rag, a quick rinse, and your skillets are spick and span again.

Many of the recipes in the saucepan sections may be made in your skillets. Your 10-inch skillet can take the place of a 1½-quart-capacity saucepan, and your 12-inch skillet can substitute for a 2½-quart-capacity saucepan. And if you wish to keep a dish warm without further cooking, you can, fill the 12-inch skillet half full of simmering water and set the 10-inch skillet into it on a small round cake rack or trivet, simulating a double boiler or what the French call a *bain Marie*.

Before giving you special skillet recipes, here's a reminder list of basic foods which you will cook in your skillets. You'll find the recipes in any good general cookbook.

French toast
Pancakes
Sautéed bacon
Pan-fried sausage cakes or breakfast sausages
Pan-fried or scrambled eggs
Pan-fried hamburgers, chops, steaks, chicken parts, ham slices
Sautéed calf's liver or chicken livers
Breaded chops and chicken parts
Pan-fried eggplant or zucchini
Sautéed green pepper strips
German-fried potatoes or potato cakes
Sautéed apple rings

Candied yams or sweet potatoes
Sautéed onions or mushrooms

Let's begin with a simple dish of ham and eggs, so good for Sunday breakfast. It also makes a delicious dinner or supper anytime. Almost any vegetable or a tossed salad and hot French bread or baking powder biscuits round out the meal. Garnish with a few fried apple rings, if you wish. You'll only need your 10-inch skillet, so put your 12-inch skillet to work sautéing the apple slices or, how about an accompanying vegetable such as candied yams (see Index)?

HAM AND EGGS FOR TWO

2 *¼-inch-thick slices*   *4 eggs*
   ham   *Water cress or parsley*
4 tablespoons butter   *for garnish*

1. Heat 1 tablespoon butter in a 10-inch skillet, and in it brown the ham quickly over moderately high heat, until just tinged at the edges with brown. Remove ham to warm serving platter.
2. Reduce heat to low. Add remaining butter and let it melt, but do not let it brown.
3. Carefully break eggs, first into a saucer, and slip them two at a time into the hot butter in the skillet. Cover and cook over low heat for about 5 minutes, or until whites are set and yolks are cooked as desired.
4. Slip eggs from skillet onto platter and garnish with water cress.

You're going to want to poach a lot of eggs, for there are so many wonderful quick dishes that you can make from them. Just on a piece of buttered toast is hard to beat, and they are also delicious served on a bed of puréed spinach, on sautéed large mushroom caps, or on mashed potatoes flavored with a little sautéed onion, and covered with a creamy sauce.

The best way to poach eggs is in a skillet.

POACHED EGGS
Serves 2

1 *quart water*
1 *teaspoon salt*
4 *fresh eggs*

1. Measure water into a 10-inch skillet. Add salt and bring to a rolling boil.
2. Break eggs into a cup or small bowl. Slip eggs into the boiling water, reduce heat to low, and let the eggs steep in the hot salted water for about 5 minutes, or until whites are firm and yolks are cooked as desired.
3. If you don't want to serve them immediately, add 1 cup cold water to water in skillet, turn off heat, and the eggs will keep warm without further cooking. When serving, trim the white neatly with a large round cooky cutter, if you wish.

And now on to some favorite meat dishes, which you will want to serve frequently. The first is a favorite with men.

BEEF 'N' BEER

Serves 4

2 *pounds California-style chuck steak*
12-*ounce can beer*
1 *small onion, grated*
2 *tablespoons chopped parsley*
1 *bay leaf*
1½ *teaspoons salt*
¼ *teaspoon pepper*
¼ *teaspoon Tabasco*
½ *teaspoon dried orégano*
¼ *cup flour*
3 *tablespoons shortening or cooking oil*
1 *large onion, sliced*
2 *stalks celery, cut into 1½-inch lengths*

1. Remove bones from steak and cut meat into thin slanting slivers. Put into large mixing bowl and pour beer over it. Add grated onion, parsley, bay leaf, salt, pepper, Tabasco and orégano. Stir to mix and let marinate in refrigerator for 6 hours.
2. Drain meat from marinade, discarding bay leaf. Reserve marinade.
3. Pat meat dry with paper towels and coat with flour.
4. In 12-inch skillet heat shortening or oil, and in it sauté meat until well browned, stirring and scraping bottom of skillet frequently.
5. Add sliced onion, celery, and reserved marinade. Bring liquid to a simmer. Cover and cook over low heat for 1 hour, or until meat is tender, stirring occasionally. Add a little more beer or water if sauce becomes too thick.

CHINESE PEPPER STEAK
Serves 4

1 *pound round steak,
cut 1 inch thick*
¼ *cup butter or cooking
oil*
1 *clove garlic, minced*
½ *teaspoon salt*
¼ *teaspoon pepper*
4 *tablespoons soy sauce*
1 *teaspoon sugar*
1 *cup canned bean
sprouts*

1 *cup canned tomatoes*
2 *green peppers,
seeded and cut into
thin strips*
½ *tablespoon cornstarch*
2 *tablespoons cold water*
4 *green onions, including
green tops, thinly
sliced*

1. Slice steak as thinly as possible into slanting pieces. This is easy to do if the steak is partially frozen before cutting.
2. In 12-inch skillet heat butter or oil. In it brown beef lightly on both sides. Add garlic and sprinkle meat with salt and pepper. Add soy sauce and sugar, cover, and cook over high heat for 5 minutes.
3. Add bean sprouts, tomatoes, and green peppers. Cover and cook for 5 minutes longer. DO NOT OVERCOOK. Vegetables should be crisp and bity.
4. Stir cornstarch into water and stir mixture into liquid in skillet. Cook, stirring, until sauce is clear and slightly thickened.
5. Sprinkle with green onions and serve with cooked rice (see Index).

BEEF STROGANOFF

Serves 2, but recipe may be doubled in same skillet to serve 4

*¾ pound round steak,
cut 1 inch thick*
2 tablespoons flour
½ teaspoon salt
¼ teaspoon pepper
*2 tablespoons butter or
margarine*

*1 small onion, thinly
sliced*
1 cup beef consommé
*1 teaspoon prepared
mustard*
*½ cup commercial sour
cream*

1. Cut meat into thin, slanting strips about 2 inches long.
2. Combine flour, salt, and pepper. Dust meat with the flour mixture, and reserve remaining mixture.
3. In a 12-inch skillet melt butter or margarine, and in it brown meat quickly on both sides. Add onion slices and brown quickly.
4. Stir remaining flour mixture into pan juices. Gradually stir in consommé, and cook, stirring, until sauce is smooth and thickened.
5. Stir in mustard. Cover, and cook over very low heat for about 1 hour, or until meat is tender. The liquid should not boil.
6. Just before serving stir in sour cream and heat to serving temperature.
7. Serve with cooked rice (see Index).

BEEF STROGANOFF WITH MUSHROOMS

Brown ½ cup sliced fresh mushrooms along with the onion slices.
Add ½ teaspoon tomato paste along with the mustard.

CHILI CON CARNE

Serves 4, but recipe may be doubled to serve 8

2 tablespoons butter or
  cooking oil
2 large onions, finely
  chopped
1 clove garlic, minced
1 pound ground beef
¼ teaspoon freshly
  ground black pepper
1 teaspoon salt
1 teaspoon ground cumin
  seed

1 tablespoon chili
  powder, or to taste
8-ounce can tomato
  sauce
¼ cup water
1 cup shredded crisp
  lettuce
1-pound can kidney beans

1.   In 12-inch skillet heat butter or oil, and in it sauté onions and garlic for about 5 minutes, or until lightly browned.

2.   Add beef, and cook, stirring, until meat loses its red color.

3.   Add pepper, salt, cumin, chili powder, tomato sauce, and water. Bring liquid to a boil, cover skillet, and cook over low heat for 30 minutes, stirring occasionally.

4.   Serve sprinkled with shredded lettuce and kidney beans on the side which may be heated in their liquid in your 10-inch skillet. Drain beans before serving.

SKILLET MEAT LOAF
Serves 4

1 pound ground beef
¼ cup chopped green
  onions
¼ cup chopped celery
1 cup fresh bread
  crumbs
1 egg, beaten
1 teaspoon salt

1 teaspoon Worcestershire
  sauce
½ teaspoon dry mustard
2 tablespoons cooking
  oil or bacon drippings
Sliced tomatoes and
  parsley for garnish

1. In mixing bowl combine all ingredients except oil or drippings.
2. In 10-inch skillet heat oil or drippings. Add meat mixture and press down well with a spoon to form meat into shape of pan.
3. Cover and cook over medium heat for 30 minutes.
4. Invert on warm serving plate, and garnish with sliced tomatoes and parsley clusters.

SAVORY MEAT PIE
Serves 6

2 tablespoons shortening
¾ cup chopped onion
½ cup chopped celery
1½ pounds ground beef
2 tablespoons flour
⅔ cup beef stock or
   consommé
¼ cup chopped parsley
2 tablespoons tomato
   paste

½ teaspoon dried basil
Dash sugar
1¼ teaspoons salt
¼ teaspoon pepper
Pastry for a one-crust pie
1 egg yolk
1 tablespoon milk

1. In 10-inch skillet *with metal handle* melt shortening, and in it sauté onion and celery for 5 minutes, or until onion is transparent.
2. Add beef, and cook over medium heat, stirring frequently, until meat loses all red color.
3. Sprinkle meat with flour and gradually stir in stock or consommé. Cook, stirring constantly, until sauce is thickened. Add parsley, tomato paste, basil, sugar, salt, and pepper, and simmer for 5 minutes. Remove from heat and cool for 10 to 15 minutes.
4. Preheat oven to 425° F. Roll out pastry in a thin circle on lightly floured board.
5. Transfer round of pastry over cooled filling in skillet. Trim off edge, leaving ½ inch overhanging. Turn overhanging pastry back under, flute, and press firmly to edge of skillet. Use scraps of pastry to cut into "leaves" for decorating pastry topping. Cut a hole in center of the pie to allow the steam to escape and arrange the "leaves" around the hole.

6. Beat egg yolk with milk, and brush pastry with the mixture.

7. Bake pie in preheated oven for 10 minutes. Reduce temperature to 350° F., and continue to bake for 50 minutes longer, or until pastry is golden.

CORNED-BEEF HASH WITH POACHED EGGS
Serves 2

4 tablespoons butter
½ cup chopped onion
12-ounce can corned-beef hash
2 medium potatoes, boiled or baked
½ teaspoon salt
¼ teaspoon freshly ground black pepper

2 tablespoons chopped parsley
4 tablespoons cream
Kettle of boiling water
2 eggs
Parsley for garnish

1. In a 10-inch skillet heat 2 tablespoons of the butter, and in it sauté onion until golden. Empty onion into a mixing bowl, and add hash and potatoes. Remove skins if potatoes are baked or boiled in their jackets. Cut through hash and potatoes with 2 knives, scissor fashion, to chop and mix well with the onion.

2. Stir in salt, pepper, parsley, and cream.

3. In same 10-inch skillet melt remaining butter. Turn hash mixture into skillet and press down evenly and firmly with spatula or pancake turner.

4. Cook over moderate heat for about 15 minutes, or until a good brown crust has formed on bottom. Cover and cook for 3 minutes longer.

5. Loosen edges of hash and fold in half, like an omelet. Turn out onto warm serving plate.

6. Pour 1 quart boiling water into same 10-inch skillet and in it poach the eggs (see Index). Arrange eggs on top of the hash and garnish with parsley clusters. Serve with catsup or chili sauce if desired.

SWEDISH MEAT BALLS
Serves 4

4 tablespoons butter
3 tablespoons minced
   onion
1 cup soft bread crumbs
1 cup milk
½ pound ground lean
   chuck
¼ pound ground veal

¼ pound ground lean
   pork
1 egg
1 teaspoon salt
¼ teaspoon pepper
4 tablespoons flour
1 cup cream

1. In a 10-inch skillet melt 1 tablespoon butter and in it sauté onion until lightly browned.

2. In mixing bowl soak bread crumbs in milk. Add meat, sautéed onion, egg, salt, and pepper, and mix thoroughly. Shape mixture into balls about 1-inch in diameter, and roll in flour. Reserve leftover flour.

3. In same 10-inch skillet melt remaining butter, and in it sauté meat balls until well browned all over. Remove meat balls to a plate or pan.

4. Stir 1 tablespoon of the leftover flour into juices remaining in skillet. Gradually stir in cream, and cook, stir-

ring, until sauce is slightly thickened. Return meat balls to sauce, cover, and cook over very low heat for 20 minutes. Serve hot.

Good with potato pancakes, which you can pan-fry in your 12-inch skillet.

BRAISED STUFFED PORK CHOPS
Serves 4

4 tablespoons butter or margarine
2 tablespoons chopped onion
¼ cup chopped celery
2 cups fresh bread crumbs
½ teaspoon salt or to taste

¼ teaspoon pepper
¼ teaspoon ground sage
¼ teaspoon poultry seasoning
4 pork chops, 1½ inches thick, cut with pocket
½ cup water

1. In 12-inch skillet melt butter or margarine, and in it sauté onion and celery over low heat for 10 minutes, or until soft. Stir in bread crumbs, salt, pepper, sage, and poultry seasoning. Mix well.
2. Fill pocket in pork chops with the bread mixture.
3. Arrange chops in the skillet and brown well on both sides over moderate heat.
4. Add water, reduce heat to low, cover, and cook chops for 1 hour, or until tender.

PORK CHOW MEIN
Serves 2

¾ pound lean loin of
pork
2 tablespoons butter or
margarine
1 medium onion, sliced
⅓ cup chopped celery
1 cup beef consommé
2 tablespoons soy sauce
½ teaspoon monosodium
glutamate

Salt and pepper
½ cup canned bean
sprouts
½ cup sliced canned
mushrooms
¼ cup sliced canned
water chestnuts
2 tablespoons cornstarch
¼ cup water
Chinese noodles

1.   Discard any fat from the pork, and dice the meat into 1-inch cubes.
2.   In a 10-inch skillet melt butter, and in it brown pork on all sides over moderate heat. Add onion and celery, and sauté for 5 minutes. Add beef consommé, soy sauce, and monosodium glutamate, and season lightly with salt and pepper.
3.   Bring liquid to a boil, cover and cook over low heat for 1 hour, or until pork is tender.
4.   Stir in bean sprouts, mushrooms, and water chestnuts.
5.   In a small bowl combine cornstarch and water. Stir into pork mixture, and cook, stirring constantly, until sauce is clear and thickened.
6.   Correct seasoning and serve over Chinese noodles.

BREADED VEAL SCALLOPS
Serves 2

*2 ¼-inch-thick slices
veal from leg,
pounded very thin*
Flour
1 egg
1 tablespoon water
*½ cup fresh bread
crumbs*

3 tablespoons butter
Salt and pepper
Juice of ½ lemon
*2 tablespoons chopped
parsley*

1.   Coat veal slices with flour. Beat egg lightly with water. Dip floured meat into egg mixture, then coat with bread crumbs, pressing crumbs into meat lightly with flat side of a knife.
2.   In a 10-inch skillet heat 2 tablespoons of the butter. Just as it begins to brown, place meat in the butter and brown on one side for about 2 minutes. Turn and cook for 2 to 3 minutes longer, or until lightly browned.
3.   Sprinkle meat with salt and pepper, and transfer to a warm serving plate.
4.   To juices remaining in skillet add lemon juice and remaining tablespoon butter. Raise skillet and swirl over heat until butter is melted. Add parsley, and cook for 1 minute. Pour pan juices and parsley over meat.

BREADED VEAL SCALLOPS WITH MUSHROOMS

Omit lemon juice from recipe above. Remove browned veal to warm serving platter. To juices remaining in skillet add remaining tablespoon butter, 1 small onion, thinly sliced, ¼ teaspoon dried tarragon, and ½ cup sliced mushrooms. Sauté for 5 minutes, or until vegetables are lightly browned. Add 3 tablespoons sherry and simmer for 2 minutes. Pour vegetables and sauce over meat, and sprinkle with parsley.

VEAL MARSALA
Serves 4

¼ cup flour
1 teaspoon salt
⅛ teaspoon pepper
1 pound veal slices from leg, pounded very thin and cut into serving portions
1 tablespoon lemon juice
¼ cup butter
1 small onion, finely chopped
¼ pound fresh mushrooms, trimmed and sliced
½ cup beef consommé
½ cup dry Marsala wine
2 tablespoons chopped parsley

1. On piece of wax paper combine flour, salt, and pepper.
2. Moisten pieces of veal with lemon juice, and coat with flour.
3. In 12-inch skillet melt butter, and in it sauté veal until lightly browned on both sides. Remove veal from pan and keep warm.
4. To butter remaining in pan add onion and mushrooms, and sauté over low heat for 5 minutes. Stir in consommé and Marsala, and bring to a simmer.
5. Return veal to pan, cover, and simmer over low heat for 10 minutes.
6. Sprinkle with parsley and serve.

SAUTEED VEAL CHOPS

Serves 2, but recipe may be doubled in 12-inch skillet

2 *veal chops, about ½*	3 *tablespoons butter or*
inch thick	*margarine*
1 *egg*	½ *teaspoon salt*
1 *tablespoon water*	¼ *teaspoon pepper*
Flour	½ *cup tomato juice*

1. Dip chops into egg beaten lightly with the water. Roll in flour and shake off excess flour.
2. In 10-inch skillet heat butter or margarine. When hot, brown the chops lightly on both sides.
3. Sprinkle meat with salt and pepper. Add tomato juice. Cover skillet and cook over low heat for 30 minutes.

VEAL CHOPS PAPRIKASH

When chops are browned on both sides, sprinkle with 1 tablespoon paprika. Add chicken broth or dry white wine instead of tomato juice, cover, and simmer for 30 minutes. Arrange meat on warm serving platter. Stir into pan juices ½ cup sour cream. Heat and pour sauce over chops.

VEAL CHOPS PROVENCALE

When chops are browned on both sides, add 1 clove garlic, minced, 1 cup canned tomatoes, and the tomato juice in the basic recipe. Cover and simmer for 30 minutes. Transfer meat to a warm serving platter. Pour pan juices over and sprinkle with chopped parsley.

VEAL BIRDS PAYSANNE
Serves 4

2 pork sausages, skins
  removed
1 cup finely chopped
  mushrooms
1 small onion, minced
½ cup fresh bread
  crumbs
2 tablespoons chopped
  parsley
1 egg
1½ teaspoons salt
¼ teaspoon pepper
8 thin slices veal,
  about 1¼ pounds

2 tablespoons cooking oil
1 medium onion, finely
  chopped
½ cup finely chopped
  celery
2 tablespoons flour
½ teaspoon orégano
¼ teaspoon thyme
10½-ounce can beef
  consommé
1 tablespoon tomato
  paste

1. Make stuffing: Combine sausages, mushrooms, the small minced onion, bread crumbs, parsley, egg, and ½ teaspoon salt and ⅛ teaspoon pepper.
2. Spread each slice of veal with a layer of the stuffing. Roll each up, jelly-roll fashion and secure with wooden pick.
3. In 10-inch skillet heat oil, and in it sauté veal birds until browned on all sides. Remove birds from skillet and to juices remaining in skillet add onion and celery. Sauté for 5 minutes.
4. Sprinkle vegetables with flour, orégano, thyme, and remaining salt and pepper. Gradually stir in consommé and tomato paste and bring to a boil, stirring constantly.
5. Return veal birds to skillet, cover and cook over low heat for 1 hour, stirring occasionally.
6. Remove birds from sauce and discard picks. Press sauce

through a sieve, or purée in a blender. Return sauce and birds to rinsed skillet and simmer for 2 minutes. Serve in the skillet.

VEAL MARENGO
Serves 6

¼ cup cooking oil
2 pounds boneless veal, cut into chunks
1 teaspoon salt
¼ teaspoon pepper
2 cloves garlic, minced
2 medium onions, chopped
¼ cup flour
1½ cups chicken broth

½ cup white wine
1 cup canned or stewed tomatoes
2 sprigs parsley
2 stalks celery, chopped
1 bay leaf
1 cup sliced fresh mushrooms
12 small onions, peeled

1. In 12-inch skillet heat oil, and in it sauté veal over high heat until well browned on all sides, turning chunks as needed.
2. Lower heat to medium. Sprinkle meat with salt and pepper, add garlic and onions, and cook, stirring, for 2 minutes.
3. Stir in flour and cook until flour is lightly browned.
4. Gradually stir in chicken broth and wine, and cook, stirring, until sauce reaches a boil. Add tomatoes, parsley, celery, and bay leaf. Cover and cook over low heat for 1 hour.
5. Add mushrooms and small onions, cover, and cook for 30 minutes longer.
6. Discard parsley and bay leaf, and serve in the skillet.

POLYNESIAN CHICKEN
Serves 6

¼ cup butter
or margarine
¼ cup cooking oil
6 serving portions of
breasts of chicken
1 teaspoon salt
¼ teaspoon pepper
2 cloves garlic, minced
1 cup chicken broth

¼ cup chopped
preserved ginger in
syrup
10-ounce can frozen
pineapple chunks
1 tablespoon cornstarch
2 tablespoons cold water
Cooked rice (see
Index)

1. In 12-inch skillet heat butter or margarine and oil. In it fry chicken over moderate heat until golden brown on all sides, turning occasionally.
2. Sprinkle chicken with salt and pepper. Add garlic, chicken broth, and ginger. Cover, and cook over low heat for 20 minutes. Add pineapple chunks, cover, and cook for 10 minutes longer.
3. Remove chicken to piece of waxed paper.
4. Combine cornstarch and water and stir into juices in pan. Cook, stirring, until sauce is thickened. Return chicken to skillet and spoon sauce over the pieces. Serve in the skillet with cooked rice.

GINGERED CHICKEN

Serves 4

3 tablespoons flour
1 teaspoon salt
¼ teaspoon pepper
½ teaspoon ground
 ginger
1 frying chicken, cut
 into serving portions
3 tablespoons butter or
 margarine

1 bay leaf
2 sprigs parsley
¼ teaspoon dried
 tarragon
1½ cups chicken broth
1 cup heavy cream

1. In paper bag combine flour, salt, pepper, and ginger. Put chicken in the bag, close, and shake to coat all pieces evenly.

2. In 12-inch skillet melt butter or margarine, and in it brown chicken portions on both sides.

3. Add bay leaf, parsley, tarragon, and chicken broth, and bring to a boil. Reduce heat to low, cover, and simmer for 25 minutes.

4. Remove chicken from pan to piece of wax paper. Discard bay leaf and parsley.

5. Stir cream into liquid in skillet and boil rapidly until sauce is reduced to about half.

6. Return chicken to skillet, spoon sauce over the portions, and serve in the skillet.

CHICKEN SUPREME
Serves 6

3 *whole chicken breasts,*
  boned and halved
Salt and pepper
2 *tablespoons flour*
¼ *cup butter*
1 *small onion, finely*
  chopped
¼ *pound fresh*
  mushrooms, sliced

¾ *cup chicken broth*
1 *cup heavy cream*
½ *teaspoon lemon*
  juice
2 *tablespoons chopped*
  parsley

1.   Pound chicken halves with side of heavy knife or with a rolling pin to flatten. Sprinkle lightly with salt and pepper and roll in flour.

2.   In 10-inch skillet melt 2 tablespoons of the butter, and in it sauté chicken for about 5 minutes on each side, or until lightly browned. Remove chicken to piece of wax paper.

3.   Melt remaining butter in the skillet, and in it sauté onion for 3 minutes or until onion is transparent. Add mushrooms, and sauté for 3 minutes longer.

4.   Add ½ teaspoon salt and a dash of white pepper. Add broth, and boil rapidly until liquid had almost evaporated. Stir in cream, and boil rapidly until liquid becomes consistency of heavy syrup. Stir in lemon juice.

5.   Reduce heat to low, return chicken breasts to sauce and cook for 15 minutes, spooning sauce over chicken occasionally. Sprinkle with parsley and serve in the skillet.

SAUSAGE-FILLED CHICKEN ROLLS
Serves 4

4 *whole chicken breasts,*
boned and halved
Salt and pepper
4 *pork sausages,*
skinned and diced
1 *medium onion, grated*
2 *tablespoons chopped*
parsley

1 *cup fresh bread crumbs*
2 *tablespoons butter*
1 *stalk celery, diced*
1 *medium carrot, diced*
¼ *cup flour*
¼ *teaspoon orégano*
2 *cups chicken broth*

1. Put chicken halves between 2 sheets of wax paper and pound well with side of heavy knife or a rolling pin to flatten.
2. Remove paper and sprinkle chicken lightly with salt and pepper.
3. Make stuffing: In a 10-inch skillet sauté sausages for 2 minutes. Add half the onion, and sauté over low heat for 15 minutes, stirring frequently. Remove from heat, and stir in parsley and crumbs.
4. Spread each piece of chicken lightly with stuffing, roll up jelly-roll fashion, and tie with string.
5. Add butter to skillet, and heat. In it sauté chicken rolls until golden on all sides. Remove chicken to piece of waxed paper.
6. Add remaining onion to butter in skillet, and sauté for 5 minutes. Add celery and carrot and sauté for 2 minutes. Stir in flour and orégano. Gradually stir in chicken broth, and cook, stirring constantly, until sauce is thickened.
7. Season sauce to taste with salt and pepper, and return

chicken rolls to skillet. Cover and simmer over low heat for 1 hour.

8. Remove chicken rolls from sauce and discard string. Keep warm.

9. Press sauce and vegetables through a sieve, or purée in blender. Rinse skillet and return to heat. Pour puréed sauce back into skillet. Replace rolls in sauce and bring just to a boil. Serve in the skillet.

GRAPE-FILLED CHICKEN ROLLS
Serves 4

4 whole chicken breasts, boned and halved
Salt and pepper
3 tablespoons butter
1 medium onion, grated
¾ cup seedless green grapes, finely chopped
2 tablespoons chopped parsley
¼ teaspoon dried tarragon
½ cup fresh bread crumbs
2 tablespoons flour
2 cups chicken stock
½ cup heavy cream

1. Put chicken halves between 2 sheets of wax paper and pound with side of heavy knife or rolling pin to flatten.

2. Remove paper and sprinkle chicken lightly with salt and pepper.

3. Prepare stuffing: In a 10-inch skillet melt 1 tablespoon of the butter. Add half the grated onion, and sauté over medium heat for 5 minutes, or until onion is transparent. Remove from heat and stir in grapes, parsley, tarragon, and crumbs. Season to taste with salt and pepper.

4. Spread chicken breasts with stuffing, roll up jelly-roll

fashion, and tie each roll with string. Roll in flour.

5. Heat remaining butter in skillet and in it brown chicken rolls on all sides. Remove chicken from skillet to piece of wax paper. Add remaining onion to skillet and sauté for 3 minutes.

6. Add stock and bring to a boil. Return chicken rolls to skillet, cover, and cook over low heat for 1 hour.

7. Remove chicken breasts from skillet and discard string.

8. Boil liquid remaining in skillet until it is reduced to almost half. Stir in cream. Replace chicken rolls and simmer for 2 minutes. Serve in the skillet.

CURRIED CHICKEN LIVERS

Serves 2, but recipe may be doubled in 12-inch skillet

12 ounces fresh or thawed chicken livers	½ teaspoon salt
2 tablespoons butter	Freshly ground black pepper
2 tablespoons minced onion	1 tablespoon flour
½ tablespoon curry powder	½ cup chicken broth
	½ cup heavy cream
	Rice pilaf (see Index)

1. Remove connecting tissues between the two lobes of each liver. Cut each lobe in half.

2. In a 10-inch skillet melt butter. Add livers, onion, and curry powder, and sauté for 5 to 8 minutes, or until livers are just cooked, stirring frequently.

3. Sprinkle with salt, pepper, and flour.

4. Gradually stir in broth and cream and cook, stirring, until sauce is thickened. Cook over low heat for 2 minutes. Serve with rice pilaf.

SAUSAGE TURKEY STUFFING

For an 18-pound turkey

1½ pounds pork
  sausage meat
2 cups chopped onions
2 cups chopped celery
2 cups chopped
  mushrooms
½ cup chopped parsley

1½ tablespoons salt
½ teaspoon pepper
2 teaspoons poultry
  seasoning
½ teaspoon sage
18 cups fresh bread
  crumbs

1. Break sausage meat into small pieces and put into a 10-inch skillet over moderate heat. Cook for 5 minutes, stirring frequently.
2. Add onions and celery, and sauté for 15 minutes, stirring frequently. Add mushrooms, and sauté for 5 minutes longer.
3. Empty vegetable-pork mixture into large mixing bowl. Add remaining ingredients and mix well.
4. Stuff turkey in usual manner.

CHICKEN-LIVER STUFFING

For 2 chickens or one 8-pound turkey

¼ cup butter or
  margarine
1 medium onion, finely
  chopped
⅓ cup finely chopped
  celery
½ cup finely chopped
  fresh mushrooms

¼ pound chicken livers,
  cut into small pieces
¼ cup chopped parsley
1½ teaspoons salt
¼ teaspoon pepper
¼ teaspoon thyme
1½ cups instant oats

1. In 10-inch skillet melt butter. Add onion and celery, and sauté for 5 minutes.
2. Add mushrooms and chicken livers, and sauté until livers lose all red color, stirring frequently.
3. Remove from heat and stir in remaining ingredients. Mix well.
4. Use to stuff chickens or small turkey.

POACHED FLOUNDER OR COD ROYALE

Serves 2, but recipe may be doubled in 12-inch skillet

1½ cups milk
1 bay leaf
1 medium onion, sliced
1 stalk celery, diced
1 teaspoon salt
¼ teaspoon peppercorns
1 pound fillet of
flounder or 1 slice cod,
about 1¼ inches thick

3 tablespoons butter
3 tablespoons flour
1 egg yolk
2 tablespoons chopped
parsley
1 tablespoon chopped
chives

1. In a 10-inch skillet combine milk, bay leaf, onion, celery, salt, and peppercorns. Bring to a simmer, and cook gently for 5 minutes.
2. Carefully place fish into the simmering liquid, cover, and poach over low heat for 10 minutes, or until fish flakes easily with a fork. Liquid should not be allowed to boil.
3. With slotted spoon remove fish to a warm serving dish. Discard skin and bones, if any. Keep warm.
4. Prepare sauce: Strain milk into a small bowl. Rinse skillet and return to heat. In it melt butter. Blend in flour,

and gradually stir in milk. Cook, stirring, until sauce is smooth and thickened.

5. In the small bowl combine egg yolk and a few tablespoons of the hot sauce. Stir this mixture into remaining sauce in skillet and stir over very low heat for 3 minutes. The sauce must not boil.

6. Correct seasoning with salt and stir in parsley and chives. Pour sauce over fish.

HADDOCK PROVENCALE
Serves 4

3 tablespoons butter
1 small onion, minced
1 clove garlic, minced
1 cup sliced mushrooms,
  fresh or canned
Pinch thyme
½ teaspoon salt
¼ teaspoon coarsely
  ground pepper

1 cup canned tomatoes,
  chopped
½ cup dry white wine
  or chicken broth
1 pound frozen haddock
  fillets
1 tablespoon flour
2 tablespoons chopped
  parsley

1. In 10-inch skillet melt 2 tablespoons of the butter, and in it sauté onion and garlic for about 3 minutes, or until onion is transparent but not brown.

2. Add mushrooms, thyme, salt, pepper, tomatoes, and wine or broth.

3. Place frozen fillets in center of skillet and bring liquid to a simmer. Cover tightly and simmer for 10 minutes. Uncover, and separate fish into flakes with a fork. Cover, and simmer for 10 minutes longer.

4. Combine remaining tablespoon butter with flour to make a smooth paste, and stir into liquid in skillet, bit by bit. Add parsley and cook, stirring, for 3 minutes.
5. Take skillet directly to table. Serve hot over hot buttered toast or biscuits.

FILLETS OF SOLE DUGLERE
Serves 4

4 *fillets of sole or flounder*
2 *tablespoons butter*
¼ *cup chicken broth*
½ *cup dry white wine*
2 *tablespoons minced onion*
1 *clove garlic, minced*
2 *tablespoons chopped parsley*

2 *ripe tomatoes, peeled, seeded, and chopped*
1 *tablespoon flour*
Salt and freshly ground black pepper to taste
Parsley clusters for garnish

1. Cut each fillet in half lengthwise. Roll each half fillet like a tiny jelly roll and secure it with a wooden pick.
2. In 10-inch skillet melt 1 tablespoon of the butter. Arrange fillets in pan, curled side up. Add chicken broth, white wine, onion, garlic, chopped parsley and tomatoes.
3. Bring liquid to a simmer. Cover skillet and let the fish poach for 5 minutes. Turn and poach for 5 minutes longer.
4. Remove fillets to a warm serving platter and discard wooden picks. Bring liquid remaining in skillet to a rapid boil. Combine remaining tablespoon butter with the flour

and stir into the sauce bit by bit. Add salt and pepper to taste, and cook, stirring, for 2 minutes.

5.   Return fillets to skillet, spoon a little of the sauce over each, and tuck a sprig of parsley into center of each. Serve in the skillet.

FILLETS OF SOLE IN VERMOUTH SAUCE
Serves 4

4 fillets of sole or flounder	½ cup dry vermouth
1 tablespoon finely chopped green onions	1 cup heavy cream
	1 tablespoon flour
¼ teaspoon salt	3 tablespoons soft butter
Dash white pepper	Minced parsley

1.   Cut each fillet in half lengthwise. Roll each half fillet like a tiny jelly roll and secure it with a wooden pick.
2.   Arrange rolls curled side up in a buttered skillet, and sprinkle with onions, salt and pepper. Add vermouth, and bring liquid to a boil. Cover skillet, and cook fillets over low heat for 5 minutes, turn, and cook for 5 minutes longer. Remove fillets to a warm serving dish.
3.   Cook liquid remaining in skillet over high heat until reduced to half its quantity. Add cream, and boil rapidly for 3 to 4 minutes, or until cream is reduced and is the consistency of light syrup.
4.   Combine flour and butter. Reduce heat and gradually stir in the butter-flour mixture bit by bit.
5.   Return fillets to the skillet. Spoon a little of the sauce over each and sprinkle with parsley. Serve in the skillet.

SALMONBURGERS
Serves 4

1-pound can salmon
½ cup chopped onion
¼ cup butter
⅓ cup salmon liquid
½ cup fresh bread
  crumbs
2 eggs, beaten

¼ cup chopped parsley
1 teaspoon dry mustard
½ teaspoon salt
½ cup dry bread crumbs
½ cup cooking oil
Lemon wedges for
  garnish

1.   Drain salmon, reserving liquid. Flake. In 12-inch skillet sauté onion in butter until transparent and golden. Add salmon liquid, fresh bread crumbs, eggs, parsley, mustard, salt, and salmon. Mix well.
2.   Shape into 4 large cakes, and roll in dry bread crumbs.
3.   Wipe skillet out with absorbent paper and return to heat. Add cooking oil, and heat. Place salmon cakes in the hot oil, and cook over moderate heat for 5 minutes, or until brown on under side. Turn carefully, and cook for 5 minutes longer or until golden on other side.
4.   Drain salmonburgers on absorbent paper and serve with lemon wedges.

SKILLET SCAMPI
Serves 4

¼ cup cooking oil
1½ pounds raw shrimp,
  shelled and deveined
½ cup butter (1 stick)
½ teaspoon salt

¼ teaspoon coarsely
  cracked black pepper
2 gloves garlic, finely
  chopped
¼ cup chopped parsley

1.   Heat the oil and half the butter in a 12-inch skillet.

Add shrimp, and sauté over moderate heat for 5 minutes, shaking skillet constantly to turn the shrimp and cook them on all sides.

2. Remove shrimp to warm plate, and sprinkle with salt and pepper.

3. To butter and oil remaining in skillet add remaining butter, and heat until butter is foaming. Add garlic and parsley, and shake skillet constantly for 30 seconds.

3. Return shrimp to skillet and continue to shake for 30 seconds longer to coat the shrimp with flavorful butter mixture.

4. Serve hot in the skillet with Italian bread to dunk in the juices.

HERBED FILLETS OF FLOUNDER

Serves 4, but recipe may be halved and cooked in a 10-inch skillet to serve 2

2 eggs
1 teaspoon salt
1 teaspoon Worcestershire sauce
¼ teaspoon white pepper
1 tablespoon lemon juice
¼ teaspoon dried dill weed
¼ teaspoon dried sweet basil

2 tablespoons minced parsley
4 medium (individual servings) fillets of flounder
2½ cups fresh bread crumbs
2 tablespoons butter
¼ cup cooking oil
Lemon wedges
Water cress

1. In a pie plate beat eggs with salt, Worcestershire sauce, pepper, lemon juice, dill weed, basil, and parsley.
2. Dip fish in egg mixture, then coat well with crumbs.
3. In a 12-inch skillet heat the butter and oil. Carefully arrange fillets side by side in the skillet and sauté for 3 to 4 minutes, or until lightly browned underneath. Turn carefully with pancake turner, and sauté for 3 to 4 minutes longer.
4. Transfer fillets to warm serving platter, or pour off excess oil and butter and serve right in the skillet, garnished with lemon wedges and water cress.

HERBED SCALLOPS

Use large bay scallops in place of the flounder. You'll need 1¼ pounds to serve 4. Rinse scallops well in cold running water and dry on paper towels. Follow recipe above.

SWISS EGGS
Serves 3

2 *tablespoons butter*	*½ cup heavy cream*
6 *fresh eggs*	*Salt and white pepper*
6 *slices Swiss cheese*	*to taste*

1. Preheat oven to 350° F.
2. In 10-inch skillet with metal handle melt butter over direct heat.
3. Break eggs into a shallow dish or pie plate and slip gently into skillet. Cook over direct heat for 1 minute, or until egg whites begin to set.
4. Cover each egg with a slice of cheese. Pour cream around eggs and sprinkle eggs with salt and pepper.

5. Bake in preheated oven for 8 minutes. Serve hot with buttered toast or halved, toasted, and buttered English muffins.

FLUFFY SKILLET RICE

Serves 4, but recipe may be doubled in a 12-inch skillet
to serve 8

4 tablespoons butter   1 teaspoon salt
2 cups water   1 cup raw converted rice

1. In a 10-inch skillet put butter, water, and salt. Bring to a rapid boil.
2. Add rice. Cover skillet tightly, and turn heat to very low. Let rice cook without raising the lid for 20 minutes. By this time the rice should be tender and all the liquid absorbed. If not, stir with a fork, cover, and continue to cook for 10 minutes longer. Fluff with a fork just before serving.

RICE PILAF

Serves 4, but recipe may be doubled in a 12-inch skillet
to serve 8

½ cup butter (1 stick)   1 cup raw converted rice
1 medium onion, minced   13½-ounce can chicken
1 clove garlic, minced   broth

1. In a 10-inch skillet melt butter, and in it sauté onion and garlic for 3 minutes, or until onion is transparent.
2. Add rice, and cook, stirring, until rice is thoroughly coated with the butter mixture.

3.   Add broth, and bring to a rapid boil. Cover skillet tightly, reduce heat to very low, and cook without raising the lid for 25 to 30 minutes, or until ready to serve. The rice can remain on the heat for a surprisingly long time without burning or drying out if the heat is kept at its lowest. Sometimes it will form a golden crust on the bottom, which is delicious.

4.   Fluff with a fork, and serve in the skillet.

TOMATO RICE PILAU
Serves 4

2 *tablespoons butter or margarine*
1 *medium onion, chopped*
1 *cup raw rice*
1 *teaspoon curry powder*

2 *cups chicken stock*
½ *cup tomato juice*
¼ *cup currants*
Salt and pepper

1.   Melt butter in 10-inch skillet, and in it sauté onion for 5 minutes.

2.   Stir in rice and curry powder, and sauté for 5 minutes longer.

3.   Add stock, tomato juice, and currants, and bring liquid to a boil.

4.   Season with salt and pepper, cover and cook over low heat for 20 minutes, or until liquid has been absorbed. Fluff rice with a fork before serving.

A skillet is a marvelous utensil in which to cook stalks of fresh asparagus which are too tall for the average saucepan. When you have a heavy skillet with a tight-fitting lid, it's great for cooking other vegetables in a small quantity

of water, such as Brussels sprouts, flowerettes of cauliflower, carrots, and so on. Because the heating surface in
a skillet is larger than a saucepan the vegetables cook
more evenly, more quickly, actually steaming, rather than
boiling, in the moist heat sealed under the cover. Try it
once; you'll like it.

Basic Method of Skillet-cooking Vegetables

Use either a 10- or 12-inch skillet, depending on the vegetable you are cooking and how many you wish to serve.
Spread the bottom of the skillet generously with soft butter, using from 1 to 2 tablespoons. Arrange whole small
vegetable, thick slices or chunks in skillet, one layer deep.
Sprinkle lightly with salt and white pepper. Add ¼ cup
water. Cover skillet tightly and cook over moderate heat
without raising the cover for 5 minutes. Check to see if
vegetables are fork tender. If not, cook for a few minutes
longer. Do not overcook. Sprinkle with chopped parsley,
chopped chives, or green onions, or with lemon juice according to taste, and serve right in the skillet.

SKILLET-FRESH ASPARAGUS
Serves 4, but recipe may be halved to serve 2

2 pounds fresh asparagus   2 tablespoons butter
1 teaspoon salt   Lemon juice, if desired

1. Break off tough white parts of the stems at a point
where they snap easily. Wash well, and peel off scales on
the stalks only with a vegetable peeler.

2. Fill a 10-inch skillet with water to a depth of about 1 inch. Add salt, and bring to a rapid boil.

3. Place stalks neatly in the skillet, cover, and boil for 8 to 10 minutes, or until stalks are barely fork tender.

4. Drain off water, add butter and turn to warm heat until butter is melted. Turn asparagus over to coat both sides with the butter, and sprinkle with a little lemon juice, if desired.

SAUTEED MUSHROOMS
Serves 4

½ pound fresh
mushrooms
3 tablespoons butter

Salt and pepper to taste
Chopped parsley

1. Wash mushrooms, and trim ends of stems. Do not peel. Slice lengthwise thinly, including stems.

2. In 10-inch skillet melt butter. Add mushrooms, and cook over moderate heat for about 5 minutes, stirring frequently. Sprinkle with salt, pepper, and parsley.

PAN-FRIED EGGPLANT
Serves 2

1 small eggplant
Salt and pepper
Flour

1 egg
2 tablespoons water
½ cup cooking oil

1. Slice eggplant ½ inch thick. It's not necessary to remove the peel unless you wish.

2.   Sprinkle slices lightly with salt and pepper, and coat lightly with flour.

3.   Beat egg and water together and pour into a pie plate. Dip eggplant slices into egg mixture, and coat again with flour, or you may use fresh or dry bread crumbs or corn meal.

4.   Heat oil in a 12-inch skillet until quite hot. Place eggplant slices in the hot oil, and fry over moderate heat for about 2 minutes on each side, or until golden.

Skillets are also great for cooking frozen vegetables, as in this following recipe.

SUCCOTASH
Serves 6

10-ounce package frozen
  baby Lima beans
10-ounce package frozen
  whole kernel corn
2 tablespoons butter
½ teaspoon salt

¼ teaspoon white
  pepper
½ cup heavy cream
1 tablespoon chopped
  parsley

1.   In 10-inch skillet bring 1 cup water to a rapid boil. Place frozen Limas and corn in the boiling water, cover tightly, and cook over moderate heat for 15 minutes, or until vegetables are just fork tender, raising lid occasionally and breaking vegetables apart with a fork.

2.   Drain off water. Return skillet to low heat.

3.   Add butter, salt, pepper, and cream. Cover skillet

loosely, and let the vegetables stew for about 20 minutes, or until almost all the cream has been absorbed.

4. Sprinkle with parsley and serve in the skillet.

CURRIED FRESH CORN
Serves 4

¼ cup butter
1 clove garlic, minced
1 medium onion, chopped
2 teaspoons good curry powder
½ teaspoon salt or to taste

2 green peppers, seeded and chopped
6 ears fresh corn, shucked
¾ cup cream

1. In a 10-inch skillet melt butter over low heat, and in it cook garlic, onion, curry powder, and salt for 5 minutes, or until onion is transparent.

2. Add green peppers, and sauté for 5 minutes longer.

3. With a sharp knife cut kernels from ears of corn, scraping cobs with back of knife to remove all corn milk. Add corn to skillet. Add cream, and cook, stirring, until mixture begins to simmer.

4. Cover skillet loosely and simmer over low heat for 20 to 30 minutes, without letting the cream boil.

SKILLET POTATOES ANNA
Serves 2

4 tablespoons butter
2 medium potatoes,
   peeled and very
   thinly sliced

Salt and freshly ground
   black pepper
1 clove garlic, minced

1.   In 10-inch skillet melt half the butter. In it arrange half the potato slices, overlapping slices to completely cover bottom of skillet. Sprinkle with salt and pepper and garlic. Arrange remaining potatoes on top. Dot with remaining butter.

2.   Cover and cook over moderate heat for 8 minutes. or until brown and crusty enough on the bottom to allow you to turn them over easily with a pancake turner.

3.   Lower heat and cook without the cover for about 8 minutes longer, or until brown and crusty on other side. Cut in half for easy serving and serve right in the skillet.

SKILLET POTATOES ANNA FOR 4

Double recipe above and make in a 12-inch skillet. After potatoes are brown and crusty underneath, cut in half or in quarters to make it easier to turn. Pick up half or a quarter on a pancake turner. Swing skillet around until it is directly opposite where the potatoes were removed. Flip potatoes over and slip them back into the place in the skillet from where they were removed. A person with a strong wrist can slip the entire 12-inch cake out of the skillet onto a large round platter, invert the skillet over them, and flip them back into the skillet browned side up. I can't, so I do it the easy way.

SWISS FRIED POTATOES
Serves 4

4 large potatoes
¼ cup butter or bacon
  drippings

1 small onion, minced
Salt and freshly ground
  pepper

1. Boil potatoes in their jackets until tender. Drain and peel immediately.
2. As soon as potatoes are cool enough to handle, cut into thin strips or coarsely grate.
3. In 10-inch skillet heat butter or bacon drippings. Add potatoes and onion, and sprinkle with salt and pepper. Cook over moderate heat, turning potatoes frequently to brown on all sides.
4. Lower heat, press potatoes firmly into a cake in skillet and cook for 8 to 10 minutes, or until a golden crust forms underneath. Turn out onto serving plate crust side up.

GERMAN POTATO PANCAKES
Serves 4

2 eggs
Dash nutmeg
1 teaspoon minced
  parsley
3 large Idaho potatoes
2 tablespoons flour

½ teaspoon baking
  powder
½ teaspoon salt
½ cup butter or
  bacon drippings

1. In large mixing bowl beat eggs with nutmeg and parsley.

2. Peel potatoes and finely grate into the egg mixture. Stir in flour, baking powder, and salt.

3. In 10-inch skillet melt butter or bacon drippings. Drop potato mixture into the hot butter or drippings by large tablespoonsful a few at a time. Fry until golden brown on both sides. Keep warm in oven until ready to serve.

STUFFED SKILLET GREEN PEPPER
Serves 6

6 medium green peppers
3 tablespoons olive oil
1/3 cup finely chopped onions
1/2 cup finely chopped celery
1 pound ground beef

2 cups cooked fine egg noodles
2 teaspoons salt
1 teaspoon chili powder
8-ounce can tomatoes
6 carrots, sliced

1. Cut slice from top of each pepper and remove seeds and membranes. Arrange peppers in 12-inch skillet, and add boiling water to come halfway up sides of peppers. Cover and simmer for 5 minutes. Drain and turn peppers upside down on rack to drain completely.

2. Dry skillet, and in it heat oil. Add onions, celery and beef, and cook until onion is transparent and beef loses all red color, stirring occasionally.

3. Stir in noodles, salt, chili powder, and tomatoes.

4. Fill peppers with meat mixture, and return to skillet cut side up. Add carrots to skillet and sufficient boiling water to come 1/2 inch up sides of peppers.

5. Cover skillet and simmer for 35 minutes. Serve peppers surrounded by the sliced carrots.

DELECTABLE STUFFED TOMATOES
Serves 6

6 *medium tomatoes*
3 *tablespoons butter or margarine*
1 *small onion, finely chopped*
¼ *cup finely chopped celery*
2 *tablespoons finely chopped green pepper*

½ *cup finely chopped mushrooms*
1 *cup fresh bread crumbs*
¾ *teaspoon salt*
⅛ *teaspoon pepper*
2 *tablespoons chopped parsley*

1. Preheat oven to 375° F.
2. Cut a thin slice from top of each tomato and reserve. Scoop out insides of tomatoes, leaving shells intact. Drain tomatoes upside down on wire rack.
3. Chop tomato pulp and set aside.
4. In 10-inch skillet with metal handle melt butter and in it sauté onion, celery, and green pepper for 5 minutes. Add mushrooms, and sauté until mushrooms become limp.
5. Remove from heat, and stir in crumbs, salt, pepper, parsley, and reserved tomato pulp.
6. Fill tomato shells with vegetable mixture, and top with reserved slices. Arrange tomatoes in skillet, cut side up. Bake in preheated oven for 20 minutes.

GLAZED APPLE SLICES TO SERVE WITH HAM, PORK, DUCK, GOOSE OR CURRIES

2 cups water   Grated rind of 1 lemon
2 cups sugar   1 stick cinnamon
Juice of 1½ lemons   8 tart cooking apples

1.   In 10-inch skillet combine water, sugar, lemon juice and rind, and cinnamon stick. Bring to a boil and simmer for 6 minutes.
2.   Meanwhile peel and core apples and cut into quarters or eighths if apples are very large. Put half a dozen wedges into the hot syrup and simmer for about 10 minutes, or until edges become transparent, spooning syrup over apples as they cook.
3.   As wedges are cooked, remove with slotted spoon to a serving dish, and continue cooking until all apples have been glazed.
4.   Pour syrup remaining in skillet over apples and cool. Cover and store in refrigerator.

PEACHES POACHED IN ORANGE SYRUP
Serves 4

1 cup orange juice   4 fresh ripe peaches,
½ cup sugar   peeled, and halved,
Grated rind of 1 orange   pitted

1.   In 12-inch skillet combine orange juice, sugar, and orange rind. Bring to a boil and simmer for 5 minutes.

2.   Arrange peach halves in syrup cut side up and simmer for 5 minutes, spooning syrup over them occasionally. Turn cut side down and poach for 5 minutes longer.
3.   Transfer peaches to serving dish, and pour orange syrup over. Chill for several hours before serving.

PRUNES IN PORT
Serves 6

1-pound package dried prunes	*½ cup sugar*
1½ cups port wine	*1 cup water*
	Heavy cream

1.   Empty prunes into a bowl, and cover with the port wine. Let soak in refrigerator overnight.
2.   Next day empty prunes and wine into a 10-inch skillet. Add sugar and water. Bring to a boil and simmer for 30 minutes.
3.   Remove from heat and cool. Refrigerate for 2 hours before serving. Serve with heavy cream.

SUMMERTIME BLUEBERRY DESSERT
Serves 6

8 slices bread, trimmed of crusts	*1 cup sugar*
1 box or 3 cups blueberries	*1 cup heavy cream, whipped*

1.   Line a 1-quart mixing bowl with bread slices, cutting

the bread into different shapes to completely line the bowl.

2.   Put blueberries in a 10-inch skillet and sprinkle with sugar. Simmer over low heat for 15 minutes, stirring frequently.

3.   Pour blueberries into prepared bowl. Top with remaining bread slices, again cutting them to fit. Place a heavy weight or a stack of saucers on top of the bread and chill for 24 hours.

4.   To serve: Unmold onto serving dish and decorate with whipped cream.

GLAZED CRANBERRIES
Makes about 1 quart

1 *pound fresh or frozen cranberries*	1 *cup water*
1 *stick cinnamon*	3 *cups sugar*
½ *cup orange juice*	¼ *cup orange curaçao or Cognac (optional)*

1.   Put cranberries into a 12-inch skillet. Add cinnamon, orange juice, water, and 1 cup sugar. Bring to a boil, and simmer, without stirring, for 20 minutes. Sprinkle with another cup of sugar and simmer for 15 to 20 minutes longer.

2.   Carefully turn berries over from bottom to top of skillet. Sprinkle with third cup of sugar and continue to cook for 15 minutes or until berries are glazed and syrup is like red taffy.

3.   Empty into a serving dish and cool. Add curaçao or Cognac, cover, and store in refrigerator, where they will keep for weeks.

QUICK CRANBERRY SAUCE
Makes about 1 quart

2 tablespoons orange
juice
1 teaspoon grated
orange rind
1 teaspoon grated lemon
rind

Dash cinnamon
2 cups sugar
1 pound fresh or frozen
cranberries

1. In 10-inch skillet combine orange juice, orange rind, lemon rind, cinnamon, and 1 cup sugar. Cook over low heat until sugar is dissolved, stirring frequently.
2. Add cranberries, and sprinkle with remaining 1 cup sugar. Cover, and cook over low heat for 15 minutes, stirring occasionally.
3. Cool and store in refrigerator.

BAKED APPLES
Serves 4

4 cooking apples
4 tablespoons brown
sugar
1 teaspoon ground
cinnamon

1 teaspoon butter
½ cup boiling water

1. Preheat oven to 350° F.
2. Core apples and peel from stem end about halfway down. Arrange apples, cored side up, in 10-inch skillet with metal handle.

3.   Put 1 tablespoon brown sugar into hole in each apple, sprinkle with cinnamon, and dot with butter. Add boiling water to skillet.

3.   Bake in preheated oven for 30 to 40 minutes, or until apples are tender. Good served hot or cold with heavy cream.

SKILLET UPSIDE DOWN CAKE

Makes 10-inch cake

¼ cup butter or margarine
½ cup brown sugar, firmly packed
6 pineapple slices
6 maraschino cherries
½ cup chopped walnuts

2 cups biscuit mix
2 tablespoons granulated sugar
½ teaspoon cinnamon
1 egg
¾ cup milk

1.   Preheat oven to 400° F.

2.   In 10-inch skillet with metal handle melt butter, add brown sugar, and stir until sugar is melted.

3.   Remove skillet from heat, and arrange pineapple slices in bottom. Place a cherry in center of each pineapple slice, and sprinkle with walnuts.

4.   In mixing bowl combine biscuit mix, granulated sugar, and cinnamon. Add egg and milk and beat on medium speed for 1 minute or 200 strokes by hand. Spread batter over fruit in skillet.

5.   Bake in preheated oven for 20 minutes, or until cake tests done. Remove cake from oven, let stand for 5 minutes, then turn upside down on serving plate.

2

———◆———

SAUCEPAN COOKERY

We hope you've been happily cooking now for several weeks—or months—with your two beautiful skillets, have turned out some exciting and appetizing meals with just these two pans, and have saved enough dollars to add both to your culinary repertoire and your kitchen wardrobe. If so, your next consideration should be saucepans in a range of sizes. Again you'll want handsome ones—ones that match your skillets, perhaps in the same color or in a complementary color.

Buy heavy saucepans that are good conductors of heat, so that foods will not stick and burn, so liquids can be kept at a low simmer or at a rolling boil, whichever you wish, without constant adjustment of the heat beneath. Heavy saucepans are not only better to cook in, and last longer, but are much safer than shiny lightweight ones that can be easily tipped over with disastrous and often dangerous results.

The two most practical size saucepans—and you'll need at least two—are a 1½-quart capacity and a 2-quart capacity saucepan. You can heat a cup of milk as easily and faster in a large pan as you can in a pint-size one, and the larger ones have infinitely more cooking potential and scope than ones that are limited in capacity. Should you need still a third saucepan for more extensive cooking or for cooking for a large family, buy still a larger size— one that is 3-quart capacity. This one is by no means essential, but is a good "extra" pan to have on hand.

1½-Quart Saucepans

You will use your 1½-quart capacity saucepan in a hundred different ways each week, but mostly for cooking frozen vegetables and small quantities of fresh compact-type vegetables such as peas. You'll use it for boiling a few potatoes and for heating enough soups or stews for 2 or 3 servings. You'll also use it for heating liquids that need to be hot before they are added to a dish-in-the-making, and for reheating gravies and sauces—not for actually making sauces, even small quantities of basic sauces. For these we're going to use your 2-quart capacity saucepan, for we're going to make them the easy way—the way a professional chef makes his sauces, and you'll need room to stir and beat.

Your general cookbook is filled with many quick canned soup combinations. We'll start with a few favorite ones.

PEA SOUP A L'INDIENNE
Serves 4

3 cups water
1 envelope green pea
  soup mix
1 teaspoon curry powder

1 cup cream
2 slices crisply sautéed
  bacon, crumbled

1. In 1½-quart saucepan combine water, soup mix, and curry powder. Bring to a boil and simmer for 3 minutes, stirring constantly. Stir in cream, and heat to serving temperature. Serve topped with a little crumbled bacon on top of each serving.

This is also delicious chilled and served cold, but substitute a topping of chopped cucumber instead of the crumbled bacon.

CREAM OF CLAM SOUP
Serves 2

Combine 7½-ounce can minced clams with 1 cup chicken broth in a 1½-quart saucepan. Stir in ½ cup cream and just heat to serving temperature. Do not boil. Serve hot, or chill and serve cold.

CORN CHOWDER
Serves 4

½ cup chopped onion
½ cup chopped green
  pepper
2 tablespoons butter
2½ cups cream-style
  corn

2 cups milk
Salt and white pepper
  to taste

1. In 1½-quart saucepan stew onion and green pepper in butter for 10 minutes, or until vegetables are tender but not browned.

2. Add remaining ingredients and mix well. Heat to serving temperature.

PUREE MONGOLE
Serves 2 or 3

In a 1½-quart saucepan combine 10¾-ounce can cream of pea soup and a can measure of tomato juice. Heat, stirring frequently, and serve with sautéed croutons.

Welsh rabbit is a good quick luncheon dish served on freshly made buttered toast.

WELSH RABBIT
Serves 2

½ pound aged Cheddar
  cheese
⅓ cup beer or milk
¼ teaspoon salt
½ teaspoon dry mustard

½ teaspoon paprika
Dash Worcestershire
  sauce
1 egg, lightly beaten

1. Shred cheese coarsely and put into 1½-quart saucepan. Add beer or milk and cook over low heat until cheese is melted and mixture is smooth, stirring constantly.
2. Add seasoning. Stir in egg, and stir briskly over low heat for 2 minutes.

The next recipe puts both your 1½-quart saucepan and your 10-inch skillet to delicious use.

SCALLOPS POULETTE

Serves 3

3 *tablespoons butter*
1 *teaspoon minced onion*
1 *pound bay scallops or sea scallops, quartered*
½ *cup dry white wine (chablis is good)*
½ *bay leaf*
¼ *pound fresh mushrooms, finely chopped*

3 *tablespoons flour*
½ *teaspoon salt*
⅛ *teaspoon white pepper*
½ *cup heavy cream*
2 *egg yolks*
1 *teaspoon lemon juice*
1 *tablespoon minced parsley*

1. In 1½-quart saucepan melt 1 tablespoon of the butter, and in it sauté onion for 5 minutes, or until transparent. Add scallops, white wine, and bay leaf, bring to a simmer, cover, and simmer for just 2 minutes.
2. In a 10-inch skillet melt remaining 2 tablespoons butter and in it cook mushrooms over low heat for about 5 minutes, or until tender. Stir in flour. Drain liquid from scallops into skillet and cook, stirring, until sauce is very thick. Add salt and pepper and cook over low heat for 5 minutes, stirring occasionally.
3. Stir in cream beaten lightly with egg yolks. Add lemon juice and parsley, and cook over very low heat, stirring, for 3 minutes.
4. Discard bay leaf, and add scallops to sauce. Heat, being very careful not to let the sauce boil.

HERBED PEAS

Serves 3 or 4

10-ounce package frozen
  peas
½ cup boiling water
2 tablespoons butter
¼ cup chicken broth
2 tablespoons chopped
  chives or green onions

2 tablespoons chopped
  parsley
Dash nutmeg
1 teaspoon sugar
½ teaspoon salt
⅛ teaspoon white
  pepper

1. Put frozen peas and water into 1½-quart saucepan. Cook over moderate heat until water returns to boiling point.
2. Drain peas, leaving in saucepan. Add remaining ingredients. Cover and simmer over low heat for 5 minutes, or until almost all liquid is absorbed.

MUSHROOMS A LA GRECQUE

Serves 4

1 tablespoon olive oil
1 tablespoon lemon juice
½ cup dry white wine
¼ cup water
½ teaspoon salt

¼ teaspoon coarsely
  cracked black pepper
1 pound small
  mushroom caps,
  washed and trimmed

1. In 1½-quart saucepan combine oil, lemon juice, wine, water, salt, and pepper. Bring to a boil and simmer for 10 minutes.
2. Add mushrooms. Cover and simmer over low heat for 10 minutes.

3. Chill well, then serve on crisp lettuce as an appetizer.

OYSTER STEW
Serves 2

1 cup milk
1 cup cream
2 tablespoons butter
12 oysters with liquid

Celery salt and white
   pepper to taste
Paprika

1. In 1½-quart saucepan combine milk and cream, and heat until steaming.
2. In 2-quart saucepan melt butter. Add oysters and oyster liquid and cook over moderate heat just until edges of oysters begin to curl.
3. Pour in hot milk, and season with celery salt and pepper.
4. Pour immediately into bowls, and sprinkle with paprika. Serve with oyster crackers.

EGG SAUCE
Makes about 3 cups

3 tablespoons butter or
  margarine
3 small shallots or green
  onions, finely chopped
3 tablespoons flour
Dash nutmeg
¾ teaspoon salt

⅛ teaspoon pepper
2 cups light cream or
  milk
3 hard-cooked eggs,
  chopped
2 tablespoons chopped
  parsley

1. In 1½-quart saucepan melt butter and in it sauté shallots for 5 minutes over low heat.

2. Stir in flour, nutmeg, salt, and pepper, and gradually stir in cream. Cook over low heat until sauce is smooth and thickened, stirring constantly. Cook over low heat for 5 minutes more, stirring occasionally.
3. Stir in eggs and parsley, and heat for 2 minutes. Serve with baked vegetable or salmon loaf or as desired.

ORANGE COMPOTE
Serves 6

6 oranges
1 cup orange marmalade
1 cup crushed pineapple
  with juice

¼ cup rum

1. Peel oranges deeply so that no white remains. Cut into segments, discarding thin membrane between each segment and the seeds.
2. In 1½-quart saucepan combine marmalade and pineapple. Bring to a boil, stirring, and simmer for 5 minutes.
3. Remove from heat and stir in orange segments and rum. Cool, then chill.

LEMON SAUCE
Makes about 2 cups

1 tablespoon cornstarch
½ cup sugar
1 cup water
Dash salt

1 teaspoon grated lemon
  rind
⅓ cup lemon juice
1 tablespoon butter

1. In a 1½-quart saucepan combine cornstarch and sugar. Gradually stir in water and mix until smooth.
2. Add salt and lemon rind, and cook over low heat, stirring constantly, until clear and thickened.
3. Remove from heat and stir in lemon juice and butter.
4. Cool and serve with lemon sponge cake (see Index) or ice cream.

QUICK CHOCOLATE SAUCE FOR ICE CREAM
Makes about 2½ cups

2 *cups sugar*
2 *tablespoons cornstarch*
¼ *teaspoon salt*
¼ *cup butter* (½ *stick*)
½ *cup light corn syrup*

⅔ *cup light cream or milk*
4 *ounces* (4 *squares*) *unsweetened chocolate*
1 *teaspoon vanilla*

1. In 1½-quart saucepan combine sugar, cornstarch, and salt. Add butter, corn syrup, cream, and chocolate.
2. Cook over moderate heat, stirring constantly, until chocolate is melted, mixture is smooth, and small bubbles appear around edge of saucepan.
3. Remove from heat. Beat well with wooden spoon, and stir in vanilla. Serve hot or cold.

2-Quart Saucepans

You'll use your 2-quart saucepan for some wonderful home-made soups and chowders, for that essential basic white sauce which ends up in a dozen different savory dishes, for a larger quantity of vegetables than your 1½-quart saucepan will accommodate, and for some luscious, old-fashioned desserts.

We'll begin with half a dozen favorite soups which will nourish two as a main dish when served with some hot bread or biscuits, or four for a "starter" course to a meal.

CREOLE GUMBO
Serves 2 or 4

6 *freshly shucked oysters*
Water
2 *tablespoons butter*
1 *small onion, minced*
¼ *cup finely chopped
    celery*
8-*ounce can stewed
    tomatoes with juice*
¼ *teaspoon monosodium
    glutamate*
¼ *bay leaf*

½ *teaspoon salt*
⅛ *teaspoon pepper*
¼ *teaspoon dried basil*
Dash cayenne
½ *pound raw shrimp,
    shelled and deveined*
2 *tablespoons raw rice*
½ *cup canned okra*
2 *tablespoons chopped
    parsley*

1. Empty oysters into a 2-cup measure and add sufficient water to make a total volume of 1½ cups. Set aside.
2. In a 2-quart saucepan melt butter, and in it sauté onion and celery for 5 minutes. Stir in tomatoes, the oyster liquid and water (but NOT the oysters), monosodium glutamate, bay leaf, salt, pepper, basil, and cayenne.
3. Bring to a boil, cover, and simmer over low heat for 15 minutes.
4. Stir in shrimp and rice, cover, and simmer for 10 minutes longer.
5. Add okra, parsley, and oysters, and cook, without boiling, for 5 minutes.

LOBSTER CHOWDER
Serves 2 or 4

2 *tablespoons butter*
1 *small onion, finely*
chopped
2 *tablespoons flour*
1 *cup water*
1 *teaspoon salt*
⅛ *teaspoon pepper*
⅛ *teaspoon Tabasco*
1 *cup finely diced*
uncooked potatoes

1 *cup heavy cream*
7¾-*ounce can lobster*
meat, drained and
diced
½ *cup cooked whole*
kernel corn
2 *tablespoons chopped*
parsley

1. In a 2-quart saucepan melt butter, and in it sauté onion for 5 minutes.
2. Sprinkle with flour, and gradually stir in water. Cook, stirring constantly, until liquid is smooth and thickened.
3. Add salt, pepper, Tabasco, and potatoes. Cover and simmer over low heat for 10 minutes, stirring occasionally.
4. Add cream, lobster, corn, and parsley, and simmer for 5 minutes.

CHICKEN LEEK SOUP
Serves 2 or 4

2 chicken legs and
    thighs, skinned
½ cup sliced leek
    (white part of 1)
2½ cups chicken broth
1 medium carrot, finely
    diced

3 tablespoons raw rice
Salt and pepper to taste
2 tablespoons chopped
    parsley

1. In 2-quart saucepan put chicken, leek, chicken broth, carrot, and rice. Bring to a boil, cover, and simmer over low heat for 45 minutes.
2. Season with salt and pepper, and add parsley.
3. Serve in large soup bowls, a leg and thigh in each plate, for two. Or remove chicken meat from bones, dice the meat, and return to liquid. Serve in soup plates to four.

TURKEY SOUP
Serves 2 or 4

1 tablespoon butter or
    turkey fat
1 medium onion,
    chopped
½ cup chopped celery
2 medium carrots, finely
    diced
2 tablespoons flour

2½ cups turkey stock or
    chicken broth
Salt and pepper to taste
1 cup finely diced cooked
    turkey meat
2 tablespoons chopped
    parsley

1. In 2-quart saucepan melt butter, and in it sauté onion

and celery for 5 minutes, or until onion is transparent.
2. Add carrots, and sauté for 2 minutes longer. Sprinkle with flour.
3. Gradually add stock, and cook, stirring, until liquid comes to a boil.
4. Cover and simmer over low heat for 25 minutes.
5. Correct seasoning with salt and pepper, and stir in turkey meat and parsley. Simmer for 5 minutes.

CREAM OF CAULIFLOWER SOUP
Serves 3 or 6

1 *medium head*
cauliflower
1 *stalk celery, cut in*
1-inch lengths
1 *medium onion,*
chopped
1 *teaspoon salt*

⅛ *teaspoon white pepper*
1 *quart good turkey or*
chicken stock or broth
Dash nutmeg
1 *cup light cream*
½ *teaspoon*
Worcestershire sauce

1. Trim stalk and outer leaves from cauliflower. Measure about ½ cup small flowerets and cook them in your 1½-quart casserole in a small amount of boiling salted water for 10 minutes. Drain and set aside for garnish. Cut remaining cauliflower into pieces.
2. Put cauliflower pieces, celery, onion, salt, pepper, stock and nutmeg into a 2-quart saucepan. Bring to a boil, then cover and simmer over low heat for 30 minutes.
3. Force mixture through a sieve, or purée in electric blender until smooth. Return to saucepan.
4. Add cream, Worcestershire sauce and reserved cauliflowerets. Heat to serving temperature, stirring occasionally.

FRENCH ONION SOUP
Serves 2 or 4

4 tablespoons butter
2 very large onions,
    thinly sliced
1 clove garlic, minced
10½-ounce can beef
    consommé
1 cup water

¼ teaspoon freshly
    ground pepper
Salt to taste
1 teaspoon lemon juice
French bread slices,
    buttered and toasted
Grated Parmesan cheese

1. In a 2-quart saucepan melt butter, and in it stew onions and garlic over low heat until onions are tender but not browned, stirring often to separate onion slices into rings.
2. Add consommé, water, and pepper. Bring to a boil and simmer for 20 minutes. Add salt and lemon juice.
3. To serve: ladle into 4 soup cups or 2 large soup bowls. Add one or several slices toasted bread and sprinkle bread generously with grated cheese.

There comes a time in every cook's life when she must make a basic white sauce, for it and its many variations are used for creamed dishes of all kinds, for creamed soups, for macaroni and cheese, for soufflés and for hundreds of different casserole dishes.

Much has been written about that lumpy white sauce, which is hard to understand, for it's one of the quickest and easiest of all recipes to make IF it's correctly made— the way the chefs make it, by using hot liquid instead of cold. This means dirtying two saucepans, but it's worth it. And, although this book is by no means supposed to take the place of a general cookbook, we're going to give you the right recipe for the basic white sauce, then tell you many delicious ways to use it. For it we'll put both your 1½-quart and your 2-quart saucepan to use.

BASIC WHITE SAUCE (Thick)

Makes 2 cups, but recipe may be divided in half to make 1 cup

2 cups milk	½ teaspoon salt
4 tablespoons butter	⅛ teaspoon white pepper
6 tablespoons flour	

1. Measure milk into a 1½-quart saucepan, and set over low heat to become steaming hot. It should begin to bubble but not really boil.
2. In a 2-quart saucepan melt butter over moderate heat.
3. Add flour, and cook, stirring, until butter and flour are thick and bubbling. Stir in salt and pepper.
4. REMOVE 2-QUART SAUCEPAN FROM HEAT TO SIDE OF STOVE. Pour in hot milk all at once, and stir rapidly with a wooden spoon, or better still a wire whisk, for about 30 seconds, or until smooth.
5. Return saucepan to stove and continue to stir rapidly over moderate heat for about 2 minutes, until mixture bubbles and becomes very thick. Be sure to stir well from bottom and sides of pan. Remove saucepan again to side of stove and continue to stir until mixture stops bubbling.

Each of the following creamed dishes uses the entire 2 cups of white sauce or its variation, to make sufficient servings for 4. Should you wish to serve only 2, all ingredients may be reduced by half. Measure out 1 cup of your basic sauce into a small bowl, cool, then cover and store in the refrigerator for another creamed dish a couple of days later.

CREAMED EGGS

Serves 4

Stir 1 cup cream into basic white sauce and cook over low heat for 10 minutes, stirring occasionally. Stir in 6 hard-cooked eggs, sliced, 1 tablespoon chopped parsley, and salt to taste. Heat to serving temperature.

CREAMED SALMON

Serves 4

Stir ½ cup cream into basic white sauce, and cook over low heat for 10 minutes, stirring occasionally. Stir in liquid from a 1-pound can salmon. Flake and stir in salmon. Stir in 1 tablespoon chopped parsley or chives, and salt to taste. Heat to serving temperature. Add a dash of dry sherry before serving, if desired.

Real honest-to-goodness chipped beef is very salty. Slice and put it into a 10-inch skillet. Cover with boiling water and let soak for 5 minutes. Drain well before adding it to your basic sauce.

The new packaged type of chipped beef, which is really sliced dried beef, needs no preblanching, and has practically pushed the true product off the supermarket shelves. Actually, it's quite good.

CREAMED CHIPPED BEEF
Serves 4

Stir 1 cup cream into basic white sauce. Add 6 ounces sliced preblanched chipped beef or packaged sliced beef (chipped-beef-type) and cook over low heat for 10 minutes, stirring occasionally. Just before serving stir in 1 tablespoon chopped parsley or chives and, if desired, fold in ½ cup commercial sour cream—makes it especially good.

CREAMED HALIBUT
Serves 4

Stir 1 cup cream into basic white sauce, and cook over low heat for 10 minutes. Stir in 2 cups cooked flaked halibut and 2 hard-cooked eggs, chopped, and heat to serving temperature. Correct seasoning with salt and a dash of cayenne. Great over a baked potato.

CREAMED DEVILED HAM
Serves 4

Make basic white sauce, but sauté 2 tablespoons minced onion in the butter for 3 minutes before stirring in flour.

Add 1 teaspoon dry mustard and a dash of cayenne before stirring in hot milk. Cook sauce over low heat for 10 minutes. Stir in 1 teaspoon Worcestershire sauce, 1 cup diced cooked ham, 1 tablespoon chopped parsley, and salt to taste. Heat to serving temperature.

LOBSTER, CRAB, OR SHRIMP NEWBURG
Serves 4

2 cups basic white sauce
½ teaspoon paprika
1 tablespoon brandy
2 cups cooked diced
    lobster, shrimp, or
    flaked crab meat

2 egg yolks
½ cup heavy cream
3 tablespoons sherry

1.   Make basic white sauce in 2-quart saucepan adding paprika along with the flour. Cook over very low heat for 10 minutes, stirring occasionally.
2.   Stir in brandy and seafood.
3.   Combine egg yolks, cream, and sherry. Gradually stir egg-cream mixture into seafood mixture, and cook over low heat for 2 minutes, stirring constantly. Do not let mixture boil. Correct seasoning with salt before serving.

The next three recipes are based on a variation of the basic white sauce.

CRAB LOUIS

Serves 2, but recipe may be doubled

2 *tablespoons butter*
2 *green onions, chopped*
2 *tablespoons minced*
   green pepper
3 *tablespoons flour*
½ *teaspoon dry mustard*
Dash Tabasco
1 *cup very hot milk*

½ *cup heavy cream*
¼ *cup shredded Cheddar*
   or Swiss cheese
6½-*ounce can Alaska*
   king crab meat, flaked
1 *tablespoon chopped*
   parsley

1. In 2-quart saucepan melt butter, and in it sauté onions and green pepper for about 5 minutes, or until vegetables are tender. Stir in flour, mustard, and Tabasco.
2. Remove saucepan from heat and pour in hot milk. Stir rapidly until sauce is smooth. Return to heat and stir rapidly for 2 minutes, or until sauce is smooth and very thick.
3. Stir in cream, and cook over very low heat for 10 minutes. Add cheese, and stir until cheese is melted.
4. Add crab meat and parsley and heat to serving temperature.

CHICKEN A LA KING

Serves 2, but recipe may be doubled

3 tablespoons butter
1 tablespoon minced
  onion
1 cup sliced fresh
  mushrooms
3 tablespoons flour
1 cup very hot chicken
  broth
¼ teaspoon salt

⅛ teaspoon white pepper
½ cup heavy cream
1 cup diced cooked
  chicken meat
¼ cup diced pimiento
1 tablespoon chopped
  parsley
2 tablespoons sherry

1. In 2-quart saucepan melt butter, and in it sauté onion and mushrooms for 5 minutes.
2. Stir in flour, and cook, stirring, until mixture is smooth and bubbling.
3. Remove saucepan from heat. Pour in chicken broth, and stir rapidly until sauce is smooth. Return to moderate heat, and cook, stirring, for 2 minutes, or until sauce is smooth and thick.
4. Stir in salt, pepper, and cream, and cook over low heat for 10 minutes, stirring occasionally.
5. Stir in remaining ingredients and heat to serving temperature.

QUICK AND GOOD CURRY
Serves 4

2 *tablespoons butter*
1 *small onion, minced*
1 *tablespoon good curry
powder*
3 *tablespoons flour*
1 *cup very hot chicken
broth*
¼ *teaspoon salt*

⅛ *teaspoon pepper*
½ *cup cream*
1½ *cups cooked diced
chicken, lamb, or duck*
2 *tablespoons chopped
chutney*
½ *cup diced cantaloupe
or honeydew melon*

1. In 2-quart saucepan melt butter, and in it sauté onion and curry powder for 5 minutes.
2. Stir in flour, and cook, stirring, until mixture is bubbling.
3. Remove saucepan from heat and pour in chicken broth. Stir rapidly until sauce is smooth. Return to heat and stir briskly for about 2 minutes, or until sauce is very thick.
4. Stir in salt, pepper, cream, diced meat, and chutney. Cook over low heat for 10 minutes, stirring occasionally.
5. Just before serving stir in melon. Let melon just heat through, but do not cook.

MUSHROOM CHICKEN SUPPER
Serves 2 (may be doubled in same saucepan to serve 4)

2 tablespoons butter or
  margarine
1 small onion, grated
2 tablespoons finely
  chopped celery
1 cup sliced mushrooms
2 tablespoons flour

1 teaspoon salt
¼ teaspoon pepper
1 cup chicken stock or
  broth
1 cup diced cooked
  chicken
Cooked rice (see Index)

1. In 2-quart saucepan melt butter or margarine, and in it sauté onion and celery over low heat for 10 minutes, stirring occasionally.
2. Add mushrooms, and cook for 5 minutes longer, or until mushrooms are soft.
3. Sprinkle mushrooms with flour, salt, and pepper, and gradually stir in stock. Cook, stirring constantly, until sauce is thickened. Simmer over low heat for 5 minutes.
4. Add chicken, and heat to serving temperature. Serve over cooked rice.

MINTED LAMB
Serves 4

2 tablespoons butter
or margarine
1 pound lean lamb, cut
into ½-inch cubes
1 medium onion,
chopped
½ cup chopped celery
¼ cup chopped green
pepper
½ cup diced carrot

2 tablespoons flour
10½-ounce can beef
consommé
2 tablespoons chopped
parsley
2 teaspoons dried mint
flakes
1 teaspoon salt
¼ teaspoon pepper

1. In 2-quart saucepan melt butter or margarine, and in it sauté lamb and onion, until meat is browned on all sides.
2. Stir in celery, green pepper, carrot, and flour.
3. Gradually stir in consommé, and cook, stirring constantly, until mixture comes to a boil.
4. Add remaining ingredients, cover, and cook over low heat for 1 hour, or until lamb is tender.
5. Serve over cooked noodles or rice, as desired.

VEAL IN TOMATO SAUCE
Serves 4

2 tablespoons butter or margarine
1 small onion, finely chopped
¼ cup finely chopped celery
¾ pound veal scallops, cut into 1-inch squares
½ cup finely chopped mushrooms
2 8-ounce cans tomato sauce
1 tablespoon brown sugar
½ small bay leaf
½ teaspoon dried basil
1 teaspoon salt
⅛ teaspoon pepper
Cooked noodles

1. In 2-quart saucepan melt butter or margarine, and in it sauté onion and celery for 5 minutes.
2. Add veal, and sauté until meat is light browned.
3. Stir in mushrooms, tomato sauce, sugar, bay leaf, basil, salt, and pepper. Bring to a boil. Cover and simmer over low heat for 20 minutes, or until veal is tender, stirring occasionally.
4. Discard bay leaf. Serve sauce over cooked noodles.

Some more good dishes from your 2-quart saucepan.

SHRIMP IN BEER SAUCE
Serves 4

1½ cups beer or ale
1 small onion, quartered
2 sprigs parsley
¼ lemon
1 bay leaf
1 teaspoon salt
2 pounds raw shrimp,
    shelled and deveined

2 tablespoons flour
2 tablespoons soft butter
1 cup tomato sauce
¼ teaspoon Tabasco
1 teaspoon sugar

1. In 2-quart saucepan put beer or ale, onion, parsley, lemon, bay leaf, and salt. Bring liquid to a boil and simmer for 3 minutes.
2. Add shrimp. Bring liquid just to a simmer, reduce heat and let shrimp poach for 5 minutes.
3. With slotted spoon remove and discard onion, parsley, lemon, and bay leaf.
4. In small bowl or cup, combine flour and butter to a smooth paste. Stir paste into the simmering liquid, bit by bit, and cook, stirring, until sauce is smooth and thickened.
5. Stir in tomato sauce, Tabasco, and sugar. Heat to serving temperature. Serve with skillet-cooked rice (see Index).

SHRIMP AND CRAB PARTY DISH DELUXE
Serves 6 for luncheon; 3 for dinner

2 tablespoons butter
¼ cup finely chopped onion
⅓ cup finely chopped green pepper
3 large tomatoes, peeled, seeded, and diced
1 pound shrimp, peeled and deveined
1 tablespoon tomato paste

1 teaspoon salt
¼ teaspoon pepper
Dash sugar
12-ounce cooked chunk crab meat
⅓ cup chopped parsley
½ cup heavy cream
1 tablespoon cornstarch
6 cooked patty shells or hot buttered toast

1. In 2-quart saucepan melt butter and in it sauté onion and green pepper for 5 minutes.
2. Stir in tomatoes, shrimp, tomato paste, salt, pepper, and sugar. Cover and cook over low heat for 10 minutes, or until shrimp are pink and tender.
3. Add crab meat and parsley, and cook for 3 minutes longer.
4. In small bowl or cup blend cream with cornstarch. Stir into shrimp mixture. Cook over low heat, stirring constantly, until sauce is thickened.
5. Spoon into patty shells.

ONION BEEF SAUCE FOR SPAGHETTI

Serves 2 (recipe may be doubled in same saucepan to serve 4)

1 *tablespoon butter or*
margarine
½ *pound ground beef*
1 *cup thinly sliced onions*
2 *tablespoons flour*
1 *cup beef stock or*
consommé
1 *tablespoon tomato*
paste

½ *teaspoon*
Worcestershire sauce
¾ *teaspoon salt*
⅛ *teaspoon pepper*
¼ *teaspoon sugar*
Cooked spaghetti

1. In 2-quart saucepan melt butter or margarine. Add beef and onions, and cook over low heat until meat loses all red color.
2. Sprinkle meat with flour, and gradually stir in stock or consommé. Cook, stirring constantly, until sauce is thickened and mixture reaches a boil.
3. Stir in tomato paste, Worcestershire sauce, salt, pepper, and sugar, and cook over low heat for 20 minutes, stirring occasionally.
4. Serve over cooked spaghetti.

MINESTRONE

Serves 4 or 6

1 clove garlic, minced
1 small onion, finely
  chopped
2 stalks celery with
  leaves, diced
2 tablespoons olive oil
1-pound can tomatoes
  with juice
13¾-ounce can chicken
  broth

½ cup chopped carrots
1-pound can garbanzos or
  chick-peas, drained
Pinch of dried sage
⅛ teaspoon pepper
Salt to taste
½ cup instant rice
2 tablespoons chopped
  parsley
Parmesan cheese

1. In 2-quart saucepan sauté garlic, onion, and celery in olive oil until onion is tender.
2. Add tomatoes, chicken broth, carrots, garbanzos, sage, pepper, and salt. Bring to a boil and simmer for 15 minutes.
3. Add rice and parsley, and simmer for 5 minutes longer.
4. Serve with grated Parmesan cheese, passed separately.

BRUSSELS SPROUTS IN GOLDEN CRUMBS

Serves 4

1 pound fresh Brussels
  sprouts
½ cup boiling water
¾ teaspoon salt

3 tablespoons butter
1 cup fresh bread crumbs
1 tablespoon lemon juice
⅛ teaspoon pepper

1. Trim bottoms of sprouts and discard any yellow or

wilted leaves. Put into a 2-quart saucepan with water and ½ teaspoon of the salt. Cover and cook over moderate heat for 15 minutes or until sprouts are just tender. Drain and set aside uncovered.

2. In 10-inch skillet melt butter. Stir in crumbs. Cook over low heat, stirring frequently, until crumbs are lightly golden.

3. Add crumbs to sprouts. Add lemon juice, pepper, and remaining ¼ teaspoon salt. Cover saucepan and cook over very low heat for 5 minutes, shaking pan frequently, to turn sprouts and coat them with the crumbs.

MEXICAN CORN
Serves 6

3 tablespoons butter
¼ cup finely chopped
  onion
⅓ cup finely chopped
  green pepper
1 teaspoon chili powder
3 cups cooked kernel
  corn

¼ cup chopped canned
  pimientos
2 tablespoons chopped
  parsley
Salt and pepper to taste

1. In a 2-quart saucepan melt butter, and in it sauté onion and green pepper for 5 minutes, or until vegetables are soft.

2. Add chili powder, and sauté for 2 minutes, stirring occasionally.

3. Stir in corn, pimientos, and parsley, and season with salt and pepper.

4. Heat to serving temperature, stirring occasionally.

CABBAGE AND APPLES
Serves 6

2 tablespoons butter
2 tablespoons flour
¼ cup water
½ cup dry red wine
1 tablespoon apple jelly
1½ teaspoons salt
¼ teaspoon pepper

¼ teaspoon ground
cloves
1 bay leaf, crushed
1 small head red cabbage,
shredded
2 green apples, cored and
sliced

1. In a 2-quart saucepan melt butter and stir in flour.
2. Gradually stir in water and wine and cook over low heat, stirring constantly, until sauce is smooth and thickened.
3. Stir in apple jelly, salt, pepper, cloves, and bay leaf.
4. Mix in cabbage and apples. Cover and cook over low heat for 25 minutes, tossing vegetables occasionally in the sauce.

SAVORY NEW POTATOES
Serves 6

1 cup chicken stock
2 sprigs fresh mint
2 sprigs parsley
1 small bay leaf
1 tablespoon chopped
chives

¾ teaspoon salt
¼ teaspoon pepper
3 pounds small new
potatoes, peeled
2 teaspoons lemon juice

1. In a 1½-quart saucepan combine chicken stock, mint,

parsley, bay leaf, chives, salt, and pepper. Bring to a boil, cover, and simmer over low heat for 10 minutes.

2.   Strain chicken stock through a fine sieve into a 2-quart saucepan. Return to heat and bring to a boil. Add potatoes. Cover and cook over moderate heat for 15 minutes, or until potatoes are tender.

3.   Drain potatoes and turn into a serving dish. Sprinkle with lemon juice.

CURRIED RICE
Serves 6

3 tablespoons olive oil
1 medium onion, finely
   chopped
2 teaspoons good curry
   powder
1¼ cups raw rice

3 cups chicken stock
2 teaspoons salt
¼ cup orange
   marmalade
⅓ cup seedless raisins
¼ cup chopped almonds

1.   In 2-quart saucepan heat oil, and in it sauté onion for 5 minutes.

2.   Add curry powder, and sauté for 5 minutes longer, stirring frequently.

3.   Stir in rice, and sauté for 2 to 3 minutes. Add stock, salt, marmalade, and raisins. Bring to a rapid boil. Reduce heat to very low, cover, and cook for 15 minutes. Remove cover and cook for 10 minutes longer, or until all liquid has evaporated.

4.   Fluff with a fork and turn into a serving dish. Sprinkle with almonds.

STEAMED WHOLE CAULIFLOWER
Serves 4

1 *medium head*
  cauliflower
½ *cup water*
½ *teaspoon salt*

3 *dashes white pepper*
¼ *cup* (½ *stick*) *butter*

1. Wash cauliflower and remove most of the tough green leaves and the hard core from bottom of cauliflower.
2. Set cauliflower, round side up, in 2-quart saucepan. Add water, salt, pepper, and butter. Bring liquid to a boil. Cover tightly and cook over moderate heat for 15 to 20 minutes, or until cauliflower is just fork tender.
3. Lift cauliflower out of pot into serving dish and pour pan juices over it.

CREAMED SPINACH
Serves 6

2 *10-ounce packages*
  frozen chopped spinach
2 *tablespoons butter*
1 *small onion, grated*
1 *tablespoon flour*

¼ *teaspoon salt*
⅛ *teaspoon pepper*
⅛ *teaspoon nutmeg*
Dash mace
1 *cup heavy cream*

1. Cook spinach in 12-inch skillet according to package directions. Drain well and set aside.
2. In 2-quart saucepan melt butter, and in it sauté onion for 5 minutes, until onion is golden and transparent.

3. Add spinach, and sprinkle with flour, salt, pepper, nutmeg, and mace.
4. Gradually add cream, and cook over low heat, stirring frequently, until mixture starts to bubble.
5. Simmer over low heat for 2 minutes, stirring frequently.

STEWED TOMATOES
Serves 4

4 large ripe tomatoes
2 tablespoons butter
1 medium onion, thinly sliced
½ cup chopped celery
¼ cup chopped green pepper
½ teaspoon sugar
½ teaspoon dried sweet basil
¼ small bay leaf
1 teaspoon salt
⅛ teaspoon pepper
2 tablespoons chopped parsley

1. Dip tomatoes for 1 minute into saucepan of boiling water. Then remove skins. Quarter tomatoes and remove core and seeds.
2. In a 2-quart saucepan melt butter and in it sauté onion, celery, and green pepper over low heat for 10 minutes.
3. Coarsely cut tomatoes into saucepan. Add sugar, basil, bay leaf, salt, and pepper, and mix well. Cover and cook over low heat for 10 minutes.
4. Uncover and cook over moderate heat for 5 minutes, to allow some of the excess liquid to evaporate.
5. Discard bay leaf, and stir in parsley.

VEGETABLE MEDLEY

Serves 4 to 6

2 tablespoons butter
1 small onion, grated
1 cup sliced mushrooms
1½ cups cooked kernel
   corn
1 cup cooked peas
2 tablespoons chopped
   canned pimiento

½ cup commercial sour
   cream
2 tablespoons chopped
   parsley
Salt and pepper

1. In a 2-quart saucepan melt butter, and in it sauté onion for 5 minutes.
2. Add mushrooms, and sauté just until mushrooms are limp.
3. Add corn, peas, and pimiento, and simmer over low heat for 5 minutes.
4. Stir in sour cream and parsley, and season to taste with salt and pepper. Heat to serving temperature, stirring occasionally.

FRUIT COMPOTE

Serves 6

¼ cup Port wine
1 tablespoon butter
1¼ cups sugar
Grated rind of 1 lemon
Dash each of cinnamon,
   mace, and nutmeg
4 medium apples, peeled,
   cored, and sliced

2 cups fresh or frozen
   cranberries
½ cup chopped pitted
   dates
⅓ cup chopped walnuts
Whipped cream or
   vanilla ice cream

1. In 2-quart saucepan combine port, butter, sugar, lemon rind, and spices. Stir over moderate heat until mixture comes to a boil.
2. Add apples and cranberries. Cover and simmer over low heat for 10 minutes.
3. Remove from heat, and stir in dates and walnuts.
4. Serve warm with cream or ice cream.

APPLES AND PLUMS WITH ORANGE DUMPLINGS
Serves 6

½ cup water
1 cup sugar
1 pound apples, peeled, cored, and sliced
1 pound dark plums, halved and pitted

1 cup biscuit mix
Dash mace
Grated rind of 1 orange
⅓ cup milk

1. In 2-quart saucepan combine water and ¾ cup of the sugar. Bring to a boil. Add apples and plums; cover and cook over low heat for 5 minutes.
2. Meanwhile make dumplings: In mixing bowl combine biscuit mix with remaining ¼ cup sugar, mace, and orange rind. Add milk, and stir with a fork just until dry ingredients are moistened.
3. Drop dumplings by spoonfuls on top of fruit in saucepan. Simmer over low heat, uncovered, for 10 minutes. Cover and simmer for 10 minutes longer.
4. Serve warm with plain or whipped cream, as desired.

BLUEBERRY GRUNT

Serves 4

15-ounce can blueberries
    in heavy syrup
½ teaspoon cinnamon
½ lemon, thinly sliced

¼ cup dark rum
2 teaspoons cornstarch
Drop biscuits
2 tablespoons sugar

1. In 2-quart saucepan combine berries with syrup, cinnamon, lemon slices, rum, and cornstarch. Bring to a boil and cook until syrup is clear and slightly thickened, stirring constantly. Set aside.
2. Make drop biscuits from recipe on box of biscuit mix, using just 1 cup of the biscuit mix.
3. Drop biscuit dough from tablespoon on top of the hot blueberry mixture and sprinkle with sugar. Bring syrup to a simmer over moderate heat. Cover saucepan tightly, turn heat to low, and cook for 15 minutes. Leave cover on until ready to serve and serve right from the saucepan.

STEWED APPLES WITH SPICED DUMPLINGS

Serves 6

¼ cup water
1 cup firmly packed
    brown sugar
¼ teaspoon ground
    cloves
¼ cup seedless raisins
2 pounds tart apples,
    peeled, cored, and
    sliced

1 cup all-purpose flour
1 teaspoon baking
    powder
⅛ teaspoon salt
⅛ teaspoon cinnamon
3 tablespoons granulated
    sugar
½ cup milk

1. In 2-quart saucepan combine water and brown sugar, ⅛ teaspoon cloves and raisins. Bring to a boil. Add apples. Cover and simmer for 5 minutes.
2. Meanwhile prepare dumplings: In mixing bowl combine flour, remaining cloves, baking powder, salt, cinnamon, and granulated sugar. Add milk and stir with a fork just until all dry ingredients are moistened.
3. Drop dumpling dough by spoonfuls into simmering apples. Simmer, uncovered for 10 minutes. Cover and simmer for 10 minutes longer.
4. Serve warm with cream, whipped cream, or hard sauce.

BLUEBERRY SAUCE
Makes about 3 cups

¼ cup water
1 cup sugar
Grated rind of 1 lemon
Grated rind of 1 orange
⅛ teaspoon nutmeg

1 box (3 cups) fresh blueberries
1 tablespoon butter
1 tablespoon dark rum (optional)

1. In a 2-quart saucepan combine water, sugar, lemon rind, orange rind, and nutmeg. Bring to a boil, then stir in blueberries. Cover and cook over low heat for 15 minutes.
2. Remove from heat, and stir in butter and rum, if desired. This is excellent served over vanilla ice cream or a slice of pound cake.

3-Quart Saucepans

A 3-quart-capacity saucepan is not essential to a beginning

cook. There is nothing special that has to be cooked in it that can't be cooked as well in a casserole of equal capacity or in a large Dutch oven, both of which we're going to recommend that you buy as soon as you are ready to add to your culinary repertoire and your kitchen cookware. It is important, however, as an extra saucepan for homemakers who are cooking for a large family, for frequent guests and around the holiday season, when one never seems to have enough saucepans.

If you feel you want to afford one at this time, even for a decorative addition to "that empty wall space near the stove," do so, by all means. You'll find it will come in handy very often for cooking bulky vegetables like potatoes, onions, cabbage; for making spaghetti sauces and main dish stews and chowders; and for simmering small quantities of homemade jams and marmalades.

Meanwhile, here are a few suggestions for putting a 3-quart saucepan to good use.

MAIN DISH CRAB CHOWDER
Serves 4

2 tablespoons butter
1 medium onion, chopped
½ cup chopped celery
1 teaspoon curry powder
3 cups diced cooked potatoes
3 cups milk
⅛ teaspoon Tabasco
1½ teaspoon salt
¼ teaspoon pepper
12-ounce package frozen Alaska king crab meat
12-ounce can cream-style corn
2 tablespoons chopped parsley

1. In a 3-quart saucepan (or casserole) melt butter and

in it sauté onion and celery for 5 minutes, or until onion is golden.

2. Add curry powder, and sauté for 2 to 3 minutes longer.

3. Add potatoes, milk, Tabasco, salt, and pepper. Bring to a boil, cover, and cook over low heat for 5 minutes.

4. Add crab meat and corn, and simmer, just until crab meat is thawed and separated.

5. Sprinkle with parsley before serving.

CREAM OF FRESH ASPARAGUS SOUP
Serves 6 or 8

1 *bunch fresh asparagus*	*Salt and pepper to taste*
2 *tablespoons butter*	*Dash mace*
1 *medium onion,*	1 *teaspoon lemon juice*
chopped	1 *cup heavy cream*
1 *quart chicken broth*	

1. Snap off tough white portion of asparagus stalks and discard. With vegetable peeler, strip scales off stalks to remove any sand lurking beneath. Soak in cold water for 5 minutes. Drain and cut off tips. Set tips aside and cut remaining stalks into 1-inch lengths.

2. In 3-quart saucepan (or casserole) melt butter, and in it sauté onion for 5 minutes. Add asparagus stalks and chicken broth. Season with salt, pepper, and mace. Bring to a boil, cover and cook over low heat for 30 minutes.

3. Meanwhile put tips in 1½-quart saucepan. Cover with boiling salted water and simmer for 10 minutes. Drain and set aside for garnish.

4. Force cooked asparagus stalks and liquid through a

sieve, or purée a couple of cuts at a time in electric blender. Return to saucepan.

5. Stir in lemon juice, cool, and chill.
6. Just before serving stir in cream and asparagus tips.

CURRY OF CHICKEN
Serves 6

¼ cup butter or chicken fat
1 large onion, sliced
½ cup chopped celery
2 medium apples, peeled, cored, and sliced
2 tablespoons good curry powder
¼ cup flour
¼ teaspoon ginger
⅛ teaspoon cayenne
1½ teaspoons salt

1 tablespoon lemon juice
¼ cup orange marmalade
1 quart hot chicken stock
1 cup seedless white raisins
½ cup sliced blanched almonds
3 cups diced cooked chicken
Cooked rice (see Index)
Toasted coconut
Chutney

1. In a 3-quart saucepan (or casserole) melt chicken fat or butter, and in it sauté onion and celery for 5 minutes, or until onion is transparent.
2. Add apple slices, and sauté for 5 minutes. Sprinkle with curry powder, and sauté for 5 minutes longer, stirring frequently.
3. Stir in flour, ginger, cayenne, salt, lemon juice, and marmalade. Remove saucepan to side of stove, and pour in chicken stock. Stir or whisk rapidly until mixture is

smooth. Return to heat and stir briskly for 2 minutes or until mixture reaches boiling point.

4. Cover and simmer over very low heat for 30 minutes.

5. Force mixture through a sieve, or purée, a couple of cups at a time, in a blender. Return to saucepan and add raisins, almonds, and chicken. Simmer for 5 minutes, stirring constantly.

6. Serve with cooked rice, toasted coconut, and chutney.

MEATED SPAGHETTI SAUCE

Makes about 5 cups

2 tablespoons olive oil	6-ounce can tomato
½ cup finely chopped	paste
onions	½ cup water
2 cloves garlic, crushed	¼ cup chopped parsley
1 pound ground beef	3 teaspoons salt
2 cups chopped fresh	¼ teaspoon pepper
mushrooms	½ teaspoon rosemary
1-pound 13-ounce can	1 teaspoon orégano
tomatoes, drained	½ teaspoon sugar

1. In a 3-quart saucepan heat oil, and in it sauté onions, garlic, and beef, until meat loses all red color.

2. Stir in remaining ingredients and bring to a simmer. Cover and simmer over low heat for 3 hours, stirring occasionally.

GIBLET GRAVY FOR YOUR HOLIDAY TURKEY
Makes 1½ quarts

Turkey giblets
1 carrot, diced
1 large onion, quartered
1 stalk celery, quartered
1 bay leaf

2 teaspoons salt
¼ teaspoon peppercorns
¾ cup drippings from
   roasting pan
¾ cup flour

1. In a 3-quart saucepan put giblets, carrot, onion, celery, bay leaf, salt, and peppercorns. Add sufficient water to come to 1 inch from top of saucepan. Bring to a boil, skimming surface of liquid occasionally to remove foam.
2. Cover and cook over low heat for 2½ hours.
3. Strain into a bowl or into your 2-quart saucepan. Add water or broth if necessary to make a total of 6 cups liquid.
4. Rinse saucepan and return to heat. Pour in drippings. Stir in flour. Remove saucepan to side of stove and pour in the 6 cups hot liquid. Stir rapidly until mixture is smooth. Return to heat and stir or whisk briskly for 2 minutes, or until mixture is smooth and thickened.
5. Cook over low heat for 10 minutes, stirring occasionally. Correct seasoning with salt and pepper if necessary.

BEEF AND VEGETABLE STEW
Serves 8, but is good reheated

2 *tablespoons olive oil*
2 *tablespoons butter or*
margarine
3 *pounds beef chuck, cut*
into 1½-inch cubes
¼ *cup flour*
2 *teaspoons salt*
¼ *teaspoon pepper*
1 *tablespoon paprika*
Dash *sugar*
¼ *teaspoon dried sweet*
basil

1 *cup beef stock*
1 *cup tomato juice*
3 *large onions, sliced*
6 *medium carrots, cut*
into 2-inch lengths
3 *stalks celery, cut into*
2-inch lengths
¼ *pound fresh*
mushrooms

1.   In 10-inch skillet heat oil and butter. Add beef, and sauté over high heat until meat is well browned on all sides.
2.   Place beef in a 3-quart saucepan and set aside.
3.   To fat and juices remaining in skillet add flour, salt, pepper, paprika, sugar, and basil. Stir well. Gradually add stock and tomato juice, and cook over moderate heat until sauce is smooth and thickened, stirring constantly.
4.   Pour sauce over meat in saucepan and add onions, carrots, and celery. Cover and simmer over low heat for 2 hours, stirring occasionally.
5.   Add mushrooms, cover, and cook over low heat for 30 minutes longer.

A Word About Double Boilers

Double boilers, more correctly known as double saucepans, are by no means necessary in a well-equipped kitchen. As a matter of fact you would seldom find a double saucepan in the kitchen of a professional chef. However, occasionally in cooking, it is a wise precaution to cook certain mixtures, such as custards and egg sauces, over hot water rather than over direct heat. Also, if a sauced dish must be held for any time before it is served, it "holds" better if it is set into a container of steaming water than if it were allowed to continue to cook over direct heat.

How is this accomplished without a double saucepan? Easy! Simply fill a skillet half full of steaming water. Set into it a small round wire cake rack or a trivet and set the saucepan containing the custard or sauced food on the trivet. The purpose of the trivet is to raise the bottom of the saucepan up from direct contact with the cooking surface of the lower pan and to allow the hot water to circulate around and under the saucepan containing the food. By such an easy method the water in the lower container is visible at all times and may be kept steaming hot or at a gentle simmer, whichever is desired. In a conventional double saucepan you cannot see the activity of the water, nor can you see the water level and, because the water is trapped beneath the upper saucepan it can build up steam and pressure, thereby defeating the purpose of the hot-water protective bath.

If a round-bottomed mixing bowl is used to cook an egg sauce or custard, no trivet is necessary in the water pan.

Here follow a few typical examples of foods best cooked over hot water.

SUMMER MEAT LOAF
Serves 6

1 *pound ground beef*
2 *cups finely diced cooked ham*
1 *medium onion, grated*
1 *medium carrot, grated*
½ *cup finely chopped celery*
1 *cup fresh bread crumbs*

2 *eggs*
1 *teaspoon Worcestershire sauce*
1 *teaspoon salt*
¼ *teaspoon pepper*
2 *tablespoons chopped parsley*

1. Grease a 1½-quart saucepan well.
2. In mixing bowl combine all ingredients. Pack into saucepan and cover saucepan with tight-fitting lid. Set saucepan into skillet of simmering water, and cook over low heat for 1½ hours, adding water to skillet as needed.
3. Cool meat loaf in saucepan, then unmold onto serving dish. Chill well and serve thinly sliced.

MUSTARD EGG SAUCE
Makes about ½ cup or enough for 3 to 4 servings

¼ *cup butter or margarine*
2 *egg yolks*
1 *teaspoon dry mustard*
1 *tablespoon wine vinegar*
1 *tablespoon chopped parsley*

½ *teaspoon crushed dried mint flakes*
½ *teaspoon crushed dried tarragon*
Salt and pepper to taste

In 1½-quart saucepan melt butter. Add remaining ingredients. Set saucepan into skillet containing simmering water and cook over low heat, beating constantly, until sauce is smooth and thickened. Delicious served with steak or broiled fish.

SAVORY ALMOND SAUCE FOR CHICKEN OR VEGETABLES
Makes 1½ cups

3 tablespoons butter	1 teaspoon prepared
⅓ cup finely chopped	mustard
blanched almonds	Salt and pepper to taste
1 tablespoon flour	1 egg yolk
1 cup hot milk	1 tablespoon dry sherry

1. In 1½-quart saucepan melt butter. Add almonds, and sauté over direct heat until almonds are golden.
2. Remove saucepan from heat and stir in flour and milk. Return to heat, and cook, stirring constantly, until sauce is smooth and thickened. Stir in mustard and salt and pepper.
3. Set saucepan into a skillet containing simmering water.
4. Combine egg yolk and sherry, and stir into sauce. Cook over low heat, stirring constantly, for 3 minutes, or until sauce is smooth and thickened.

CHOCOLATE SAUCE
Makes about 1 quart

2 squares unsweetened	2 teaspoons cornstarch
chocolate (2 ounces)	4 egg yolks
3 cups milk	Dash salt
¼ cup sugar	

1. In 1½-quart saucepan, put chocolate and 1 cup of the milk. Heat in skillet of simmering water until chocolate is melted.
2. In a small bowl combine sugar and cornstarch. Add egg yolks and beat until mixture is smooth. Gradually stir in remaining 2 cups milk.
3. Stir egg mixture into chocolate mixture, add salt, and cook over simmering water for about 10 minutes, stirring frequently, until sauce is thick and smooth.
4. Serve with ice cream or on baked chocolate pudding as desired.

LEMON BUTTER
Makes about 1½ pints

4 lemons	*1⅓ cups sugar*
½ cup butter (1 stick)	*4 eggs, beaten*
Dash salt	

1. Grate rind of 3 lemons. Squeeze juice from all lemons to make a total of ½ cup juice.
2. In 1½-quart saucepan put butter. Set saucepan into skillet of simmering water and let butter melt.
3. Add lemon rind, lemon juice, salt, sugar, and eggs.
4. Cook over barely simmering water, stirring constantly, until mixture is thickened and smooth.
5. Pour into jars. Cool, cover and store in refrigerator. Use as filling for tart shells or baked pie. It's great simply spread on hot toast or serve with hot biscuits.

LEMON SOUFFLES
Serves 6

1 envelope plain gelatin
⅔ cup sugar
¼ cup water
Juice and grated rind of
  3 lemons

3 eggs, separated
1 cup heavy cream,
  whipped

1. In 1½-quart saucepan combine gelatin, ⅓ cup of the sugar, and water. Set saucepan into skillet containing hot water, and stir until gelatin is thoroughly dissolved. Empty mixture into mixing bowl. Stir in lemon juice and rind and let cool.
2. In same saucepan mix egg yolks with remaining ⅓ cup sugar. Return to skillet containing hot water, and cook with water at a simmer for about 5 minutes, beating constantly, until mixture becomes thickened and pale in color. Stir egg mixture into gelatin mixture and chill until it begins to set.
3. Beat egg whites until stiff but not dry. Fold beaten egg whites and whipped cream into the lemon custard. Spoon into 6 individual serving dishes and chill until firm. If desired, decorate with additional whipped cream.

ORANGE SABAYON SAUCE
Serves 3

4 egg yolks
¼ cup sugar
Grated rind and juice of 1 orange

1. In 1½-quart saucepan combine egg yolks and sugar. Place saucepan in skillet containing simmering water. Keep water at a simmer and, with a wire whisk, beat mixture for about 5 minutes, or until frothy and slightly thickened.
2. Remove from heat and strain into serving dish. Stir in orange rind and juice.
3. Serve with fruit salad or with Christmas pudding.

PEARS A LA JOANNE
Serves 8

⅓ cup sugar
¼ cup cornstarch
Dash salt
5 egg yolks (use whites to make meringues)
1½ cups milk
1 tablespoon grated orange rind

3 tablespoons orange juice
8 meringue shells
8 pear halves, peeled fresh or canned and well drained
Whipped cream

1. In 1½-quart saucepan combine sugar and cornstarch. Add salt, and gradually beat in egg yolks to make a smooth paste. Gradually stir in milk.
2. Set saucepan into a skillet of simmering water and cook over low heat, stirring constantly, until sauce is smooth and thickened.
3. Strain sauce into a mixing bowl and stir in orange rind and juice. Cool.
4. Just before serving time, spoon the orange cream into meringue shells, top each with half a pear, and decorate with whipped cream.

ZABAGLIONE
Serves 2 or 3

4 egg yolks
⅓ cup sugar
Dash salt

⅓ cup Marsala wine or
sweet sherry

1.   In 1½-quart saucepan beat egg yolks. Gradually beat in sugar, salt, and wine.
2.   Set saucepan into skillet containing simmering water, and beat constantly over low heat until mixture is very foamy and slightly thickened.
3.   Spoon into serving dishes and serve warm.

CREME BRULEE
Serves 6

4 tablespoons sugar
1 tablespoon cornstarch
6 egg yolks
3 cups hot heavy cream

2 teaspoons vanilla
extract
1½ cups confectioners'
sugar

1.   In 1½-quart saucepan combine sugar, cornstarch, and egg yolks. Beat with rotary beater for 2 or 3 minutes, or until mixture is thick and pale in color. Gradually beat in cream.
2.   Set saucepan into skillet containing simmering water and cook over low heat, stirring constantly with a wooden spoon, until mixture is thick enough to coat the spoon. Do not let water in skillet boil.

3. Stir in vanilla and pour cream into a serving bowl. Chill for several hours or overnight.

4. When cream is cold and set, measure confectioners' sugar into a 12-inch skillet. Stir constantly with a wooden spoon over moderate heat until sugar is melted and has turned to a golden syrup. Pour the hot syrup over surface of the chilled cream. Use a rubber spatula, if necessary, to spread it to the edge of dish. Chill again until ready to serve.

3

OPEN BAKERS
OR ROASTING PANS
ARE VERSATILE

So far, if you've been "cooking along" with this book, you've been concentrating on top-of-the-stove cookery. But you've got a good oven sitting there, and it's about time to put it to use. We hope we've allowed enough time for your budget to permit buying at least one or preferably two oven baking dishes.

The deep, lightweight roaster with its high dome cover is obsolete. In its place are heavy-duty shallow open roasting or baking pans in a variety of sizes. They are usually oblong and about 2 inches deep and may be used for many other cooking purposes than just roasting.

Two different-size open bakers are most practical for the average family. These are, a small open baker about 10×6×2 inches, and a large open baker 14×8½×2 inches. The capacity of the small baker is just exactly half that of the large baker, so that any recipe given for the small baker may be doubled and baked in the larger baker when you wish to cook for a large number of people. By selecting handsome and colorful open bakers you can, in many instances, take your new cookware directly from stove to table.

The small open baker (10×6×2) is perfect for small rolled roasts, for 2 or 3 Rock Cornish game hens or for a small roasting chicken. It's a wonderfully handy size for scalloped potatoes, candied sweet potatoes, macaroni and cheese, vegetables au gratin, and so on. It may also be used for deep-dish fruit pies and for one-layer cakes. Any cake recipe specifying one 8-inch layer may be baked in your small open baker.

The larger open baker ($14 \times 8\frac{1}{2} \times 2$), or lasagne dish, is big enough for most family roasting uses and takes a small turkey, a duck, a rolled roast of beef, or a small leg of lamb and, as we said, may be used for party cooking by doubling any recipe designed for the smaller size baker. Any cake recipe specifying three 8-inch layers may be baked in one layer in the large baker. Baking temperature would remain the same, but baking time would increase to 50 or 60 minutes. When adapting a cake recipe to a different pan it's best to use a cake tester to determine when it is ready to come out of the oven. When the tester comes out clean, the cake is done. But there are many cake recipes and refrigerator desserts that call for a large oblong cake pan for which you may use your large open baker.

Unless you are cooking daily for an exceptionally large family or during the holiday season, when you might want to try your hand at a very large turkey, a goose, a whole ham, or a large rack of pork, these two sizes of open bakers are more than adequate. And since it does not seem practical to recommend buying a very large roaster just for special-occasion roasts, we suggest when the time comes that you feel you need and can afford a third and very large roasting pan, you consider one that is handsome enough to use for stove-to-table cooking or as a large serving dish for the party buffet table. There is one available, for instance, a beautifully designed round open roaster about 14 inches in diameter, with a capacity of $3\frac{1}{2}$ quarts, that is porcelainized cast iron in lovely decorator's colors. It is sometimes known as a paella dish, for paella is one of the many party foods for which this elegant piece of cookware was designed. It is also great for the buffet service of such dishes as Beef Stroganoff, Veal Birds in Wine Sauce, Meat Balls in Gravy, Spaghetti with Meat Sauce, Chicken Paprikash, curried shrimp or chicken, and even party desserts such as poached or baked fruits or a big colorful pyramid of scoops of various flavored ice creams, topped with a dessert sauce and chopped nuts. You can use it to roast or bake in, serve in and as a decorative addition to your kitchen. You can even use it as a baking surface for cookies, shortbread, or biscuits.

So shop around before investing in roasting pans and open bakers. Buy wisely and well, and your new oven cookware will give you pleasure for many years.

Small Open Baker

APPLED PORK ROAST
Serves 6

1 cup applesauce	1½ teaspoons salt
1 small onion, grated	¼ teaspoon pepper
2 teaspoons prepared mustard	3-pound boneless rolled loin of pork

1. Mix applesauce with onion, mustard, salt, and pepper.
2. Put pork roast in a small open baking dish (10× 6×2 inches), and spread applesauce mixture over it. Let pork stand at room temperature for about 2 hours.
3. Preheat oven to 325° F.

4. Roast pork in preheated oven for 2½ hours, or until meat thermometer registers 185° F.

ROLLED ROAST OF BEEF WITH VEGETABLES
Serves 4

3½-pound boned rolled
   roast of beef
Flour
1 teaspoon salt
¼ teaspoon coarsely
   ground pepper
¼ teaspoon dried thyme,
   orégano, or tarragon

8 small carrots
4 medium potatoes
4 medium onions
1½ cups beef consommé
   or broth

1. Preheat oven to 325° F.
2. Rub roast with flour. Insert meat thermometer, if desired, into center of meat. Place in open baking dish (10×6×2 inches) and sprinkle with salt, pepper, and herbs. Roast in preheated oven until done to taste:

> About 2 hours for rare, or 140° F. on thermometer
> About 2½ hours for medium, or 160° F. on thermometer
> About 3 hours for well done, or 170° F. on thermometer

3. While meat is roasting, scrape carrots and split lengthwise; peel potatoes and onions. Put vegetables into a 2-quart saucepan with enough salted water to cover. Bring to a boil and cook for 15 minutes. Drain.
4. A half hour before meat is done, arrange vegetables

around meat and baste well with juices in roasting pan.
5. When meat and vegetables are done, remove baker to
top of stove. Place meat in center of a warm serving platter
and surround by vegetables. Set in a warm place.
6. Make gravy: Stir 2 tablespoons flour into fat and juices
in baker. Gradually stir in consommé or broth, and cook,
stirring constantly, until gravy is smooth and thickened.
Cook for 5 minutes, stirring occasionally. Correct seasoning
with salt and pepper and strain into sauceboat. Serve gravy
separately from meat and vegetables.

SAVORY PORK CHOPS
Serves 6

2 tablespoons butter or margarine	½ cup chopped green pepper
6 loin pork chops, about ¾ inch thick	1 cup sliced mushrooms
Salt and pepper	8-ounce can tomato sauce
1 medium onion, chopped	¼ teaspoon dried thyme
	Dash mace

1. Preheat oven to 350° F. Lightly grease an open baking
dish (10×6×2 inches).
2. In 10-inch skillet melt butter or margarine, and in it
brown chops well on both sides. Arrange chops in baking
dish and sprinkle with salt and pepper.
3. Add onion and green pepper to fat remaining in skillet
and cook over low heat for 5 minutes, or until partially
tender. Add mushrooms, tomato sauce, thyme, mace, and

salt and pepper to taste. Bring mixture to a boil, then pour over chops.

4. Cover baking dish with aluminum foil and bake in preheated oven for 1 hour. Serve chops with the sauce in the baker.

CRAB-STUFFED FLOUNDER
Serves 6

¼ cup butter
1 medium onion, grated
⅓ cup flour
½ teaspoon salt
⅛ teaspoon pepper
⅛ teaspoon mace
Dash cayenne
½ cup milk
1 cup flaked cooked crab meat

¼ cup chopped parsley
6 large fillets of flounder or haddock
Lemon juice
1 egg yolk
1 cup light cream
⅓ cup grated Parmesan cheese

1. Preheat oven to 350° F. Grease open baking dish (10× 6×2 inches).

2. In 1½-quart saucepan melt butter, and in it sauté onion for 5 minutes, until onion is transparent but not brown. Stir in flour, salt, pepper, mace, and cayenne. Gradually stir in milk, and cook over low heat, stirring constantly, until sauce is smooth and thickened. Remove sauce from heat.

3. In a small bowl combine ⅓ cup of the sauce with crab meat and parsley. Spread crab mixture on half of each fillet. Fold fillet over and secure with wooden pick.

4. Arrange fish in baking dish, sprinkle with lemon juice and cover with aluminum foil. Bake in preheated oven for 30 minutes.

5. Remove fish from oven and drain off excess liquid into sauce. Combine egg yolk and cream and stir into sauce. Add cheese and cook over low heat, stirring constantly, until cheese is melted and sauce is smooth. Do not let sauce boil.

6. Pour sauce over fish in baking dish, and broil 5 inches from source of heat for 5 minutes, or until bubbly and golden. Serve right in baking dish.

BROILED SCALLOPS
Serves 6

⅓ cup butter
1 tablespoon chopped chives
1 tablespoon chopped parsley
1 tablespoon lemon juice
1 teaspoon salt
⅛ teaspoon pepper
1 teaspoon Worcestershire sauce
2 pounds bay scallops

1. Preheat broiler. Grease an open baking dish (10×6×2 inches).

2. Melt butter in a 1½-quart saucepan or 10-inch skillet and stir in chives, parsley, lemon juice, salt, pepper, and Worcestershire sauce. Arrange scallops in baking dish and sprinkle with butter mixture.

3. Broil scallops 4 to 5 inches from source of heat for 5 to 7 minutes, turning scallops occasionally. Serve right from baking dish.

SALMON CAPERS
Serves 6

6 salmon steaks, about
  6 ounces each
Salt and pepper
1 tablespoon lemon juice
⅓ cup butter
⅓ cup flour
1¼ cups milk
⅛ teaspoon dried dill
  weed

1 tablespoon chopped
  capers
1 hard-cooked egg, diced
2 tablespoons chopped
  parsley
⅓ cup dry bread
  crumbs

1. Preheat oven to 375° F. Grease an open baking dish (10×6×2 inches).

2. Arrange salmon steaks in baking dish and sprinkle with salt and pepper. Sprinkle with lemon juice. Cover with foil and bake in preheated oven for 30 minutes.

3. While salmon is cooking prepare sauce: In 2-quart saucepan melt butter. Blend in flour. Gradually stir in milk, and cook over moderate heat, stirring constantly, until sauce is smooth and thickened. Season to taste with salt and pepper, and stir in dill, capers, egg, and parsley.

4. Remove salmon from oven and drain excess liquid into sauce. Turn oven to broil. Spread sauce over salmon steaks and sprinkle with crumbs.

5. Broil 5 inches from source of heat for 4 to 5 minutes, or until bubbly and golden. Serve right from baking dish.

SALMON ROMANOFF
Serves 4

*½ cup finely chopped
green onion*
1 clove garlic, minced
2 tablespoons butter
1 cup cottage cheese
2 cups sour cream
5 dashes Tabasco

½ teaspoon salt
1-pound can salmon
*6 ounces medium
noodles*
*1 cup shredded Cheddar
cheese*

1. In 10-inch skillet sauté onion and garlic in butter until onion is transparent and tender. Empty into large mixing bowl.
2. Stir in cottage cheese, sour cream, Tabasco, and salt. Stir in liquid from can of salmon. Flake and add salmon. Mix lightly.
3. Preheat oven to 325° F. Grease open baker (10×6×2 inches).
4. Cook noodles in 3-quart saucepan according to package directions. Drain and stir into salmon mixture.
5. Turn mixture into baking dish and sprinkle with shredded cheese. Bake in preheated oven for 30 minutes, or until cheese is melted and lightly brown.

DELECTABLE SWORDFISH
Serves 6

3 tablespoons butter
3 small shallots or green
  onions, finely chopped
2 tablespoons chopped
  parsley
1 teaspoon salt

⅛ teaspoon pepper
Dash Tabasco
Juice of 1 lemon
½ cup dry white wine
2 pounds swordfish steak,
  cut 1 inch thick

1. Preheat oven to 250° F. Grease open baker (10×6×2 inches).
2. In 1½-quart saucepan melt butter and in it cook shallots or green onions over low heat for 5 minutes. Remove from heat, and stir in parsley, salt, pepper, Tabasco, lemon juice, and wine.
3. Arrange swordfish in prepared pan and pour wine mixture over it.
4. Bake in preheated oven for 20 minutes, or until fish flakes easily when tested with a fork, basting every 5 minutes with juices in the pan. Serve right from baking dish.

LEMON CHICKEN
Serves 4

¼ cup olive or cooking
  oil
Juice and grated rind of
  1 lemon
1 clove garlic, minced
¼ teaspoon thyme or
  tarragon

1 teaspoon salt
¼ teaspoon pepper
3½ pound broiler-fryer,
  cut into serving pieces
¼ cup butter
2 tablespoons minced
  parsley

1. Put oil, lemon juice, lemon rind, garlic, thyme or tarragon, salt, and pepper in bottom of a small open baker (10×6×2 inches). Mix well with a fork.
2. Dip chicken pieces on both sides in lemon mixture, and marinate for at least 4 hours, turning once.
3. Preheat oven to 350° F.
4. Dot chicken pieces with butter. Bake in preheated oven for 45 minutes, basting occasionally with juices in dish.
5. Serve right from baking dish, sprinkled with parsley. Good with curried rice (see Index).

QUICHE LORRAINE
Serves 6

Pastry for a 1-crust pie	*1 tablespoon flour*
½ pound bacon, diced	*¾ teaspoon salt*
1 small onion, finely	*⅛ teaspoon pepper*
chopped	*¼ teaspoon dry mustard*
2 cups shredded Cheddar,	*4 eggs, beaten*
Swiss or Gruyere	*1 cup milk*
cheese	*1 cup heavy cream*

1. Roll out pastry thinly into a rectangle and line a small open baker (10×6×2 inches). Turn back edge and flute against edge of baker.
2. Preheat oven to 400° F.
3. Sauté bacon in 10-inch skillet for 5 minutes. Add onion, and continue to sauté until bacon is crisp and onion is transparent. Drain on absorbent paper, then sprinkle onto bottom of prepared baker.
4. Toss cheese lightly with flour, salt, pepper, and mustard. Sprinkle cheese mixture on top of bacon and onion.

5.   Combine eggs with milk and cream, and pour into baker.
6.   Bake in preheated oven for 10 minutes. Reduce oven temperature to 350° F. and bake for 30 minutes longer, of until filling is firm.

EGGPLANT PARMIGIANA
Serves 6

1 *large eggplant*	½ *teaspoon dried sweet*
Salt	*basil*
Olive oil	¼ *teaspoon dried*
1 *medium onion, finely*	*orégano*
chopped	Salt *and* pepper *to taste*
1-*pound can tomatoes*	1½ *cups fresh bread*
1 *clove garlic, minced*	*crumbs*
2 *tablespoons tomato*	⅓ *cup grated Parmesan*
paste	*cheese*
2 *tablespoons chopped*	8 *ounces Mozzarella*
parsley	*cheese, thinly sliced*

1.   Slice eggplant crosswise about ⅜ inch thick. Stack slices on drainboard, sprinkling each lightly with salt. Let stand for 30 minutes, then rinse and pat each slice dry.
2.   In 12-inch skillet heat about 3 tablespoons oil, and in it sauté eggplant slices until lightly browned on each side. Set slices aside on absorbent paper to drain as they brown, and add more oil to skillet as needed.
3.   Preheat oven to 400° F.
4.   In 2-quart saucepan heat 2 tablespoons oil, and in it

sauté onion for 5 minutes. Stir in undrained tomatoes, garlic, tomato paste, parsley, basil, and orégano. Season well with salt and pepper. Bring to a boil and simmer over low heat for 20 minutes.

5. Assemble dish: Combine crumbs and cheese. Arrange alternate layers of eggplant, tomato sauce, crumbs, and Mozzarella cheese in prepared pan, ending with cheese.

6. Bake in preheated oven for 20 minutes, or until cheese is melted and sauce is bubbling.

LEMON CANDIED YAMS

Serves 6

*6 medium yams or
sweet potatoes, boiled,
peeled, and quartered*
*3 tablespoons butter or
margarine*
⅓ cup light corn syrup

*Grated rind and juice of
1 lemon*
Dash mace
Dash nutmeg
½ cup chopped walnuts

1. Preheat oven to 375° F. Butter open baker (10×6×2 inches). Arrange yams in bottom of pan.

2. In 1½-quart saucepan melt butter or margarine. Remove from heat and stir in corn syrup, lemon rind, lemon juice, mace, and nutmeg.

3. Pour butter mixture over yams and sprinkle with walnuts.

4. Bake in preheated oven for 20 to 30 minutes.

TOMATOES PROVENCALE

Serves 6

3 tablespoons butter
1 small clove garlic,
　minced
Salt
⅛ teaspoon pepper
½ cup fresh bread
　crumbs

¼ cup grated Parmesan
　cheese
2 tablespoons chopped
　parsley
4 medium tomatoes

1.　Grease open baker (10×6×2 inches). Preheat oven to 375° F.
2.　In 10-inch skillet melt butter and in it cook garlic over low heat for 2 minutes without letting garlic brown. Remove skillet from heat and stir in salt, pepper, crumbs, cheese, and parsley.
3.　Wash tomatoes and cut in half. Arrange tomato halves, cut side up, in prepared pan. Sprinkle lightly with salt. Sprinkle with crumb mixture.
4.　Bake in preheated oven for 15 minutes.

OVEN RISOTTO

Serves 4 to 6

3 tablespoons butter
1 medium onion, finely
　chopped
1 cup raw rice

¼ teaspoon saffron
1 teaspoon salt
¼ teaspoon pepper
2½ cups chicken stock

1.　Preheat oven to 350° F.

2. Place open baker (10×6×2 inches) directly over moderate heat. In it melt butter and sauté onion for 5 minutes, or until onion is golden. Stir in rice and sauté for 5 minutes longer, stirring frequently.

3. Add saffron, salt, pepper, and stock, and bring to a boil.

4. Transfer baking dish to preheated oven and bake for 25 minutes, or until most of the liquid has been absorbed. Fluff with a fork and serve right in baking dish.

CREAMY STUFFED POTATOES
Serves 6

6 medium baking potatoes

3 tablespoons chopped chives or green onion tops

3 tablespoons chopped parsley

¾ cup commercial sour cream

½ teaspoon Worcestershire sauce

Salt and pepper

¼ cup grated Parmesan cheese

1. Preheat oven to 375° F.

2. Wash potatoes well and prick each in several places to allow steam to escape. Place on rack in preheated oven and bake for 45 minutes.

3 Cut a slice from top of each potato and scoop out insides, keeping skins intact. Mash potato insides, and beat in chives, parsley, sour cream, and Worcestershire sauce. Season to taste with salt and pepper.

4. Fill potato skins with potato mixture and arrange in an open baker (10×6×2 inches). Sprinkle potatoes with

cheese and bake in preheated oven for 15 minutes, or until cheese is lightly browned.

MACARONI AND CHEESE
Serves 6

8 ounces elbow macaroni
2 tablespoons butter
2 tablespoons flour
2 cups milk

2½ cups shredded or diced Cheddar cheese
⅛ teaspoon coarsely ground pepper
½ cup fresh bread crumbs

1. Fill 3-quart saucepan with 2 quarts water. Add 2 teaspoons salt and bring to a rapid boil. Gradually add macaroni without letting water stop boiling, and boil rapidly for 10 minutes. Drain through a sieve and rinse macaroni well in cold water.

2. Preheat oven to 375° F. Grease open baker (10×6×2 inches).

3. In 2-quart saucepan melt butter. Stir in flour. Gradually stir in milk and cook, stirring, until sauce is smooth and thickened. Add 2 cups of the cheese and pepper and stir over moderate heat until cheese is melted.

4. Empty cooked macaroni into baking dish. Pour sauce over the macaroni. Combine bread crumbs with remaining ½ cup cheese and sprinkle over top of macaroni and sauce.

5. Bake in preheated oven for 30 minutes. Serve right from baking dish.

POTATOES BAKED IN CREAM
Serves 4 to 6

4 cups thinly sliced
   potatoes
1 clove garlic, minced
   (optional)

Salt and coarsely ground
   pepper to taste
2 cups light cream

1. Preheat oven to 325° F. Grease open baker (10×
6×2 inches).
2. Arrange half the potatoes in baking pan. Sprinkle with
garlic, salt, and pepper. Cover with remaining potatoes.
3. Add cream. If there is not enough to just cover potatoes, add a little milk. Put baking pan over direct heat
and bring liquid to a simmer.
4. Transfer pan to preheated oven and bake for 1½ hours.
Serve right from baking dish.

CAULIFLOWER AU GRATIN
Serves 4 to 6

2 cups water
1 medium head
   cauliflower, cut into
   flowerettes
½ cup butter (1 stick)
6 tablespoons flour
2 cups hot milk
1 cup light cream

1 teaspoon salt
   (approximately)
Dash white pepper
2 tablespoons grated
   Parmesan cheese
½ cup fresh bread
   crumbs

1. Put water and ½ teaspoon salt into 2-quart saucepan

and bring water to a boil. Add cauliflowerettes, cover, and cook over low heat for 10 minutes, or until cauliflower is just fork tender. Drain well and empty into greased open baker (10×6×2 inches).

2. Preheat oven to 375° F.

3. In 2-quart saucepan melt 6 tablespoons of the butter. Stir in flour, and cook, stirring, until mixture is smooth and bubbling. Remove saucepan from heat. Add hot milk, all at once, and stir vigorously until smooth. Return to heat and cook, stirring well from bottom and sides of pan, for about 3 minutes, or until sauce is thickened. Stir in light cream, about 1 teaspoon salt, or to taste, and dash white pepper. Cook over low heat for 5 minutes, stirring occasionally. Pour over cauliflower in baker.

4. Melt remaining 2 tablespoons butter and mix with cheese and crumbs. Sprinkle crumb mixture over top of sauce.

5. Bake in preheated oven for 20 minutes, or until top is crusty and golden. Serve right in the baking dish.

BROCCOLI LUNCHEON DISH
Serves 4

10-ounce package frozen
   broccoli or 1 bunch
   fresh broccoli, cooked
4 slices cooked ham or
   chicken
2 cups medium cream
   sauce

½ cup shredded cheese
2 teaspoons prepared
   mustard
1 teaspoon salt
1 tablespoon minced
   onion

1. Arrange broccoli in bottom of small open baker (10×
6×2 inches).
2. Place ham or chicken slices over the broccoli.
3. Preheat oven to 400° F.
4. In saucepan combine cream sauce, cheese, mustard,
salt, and onion, and cook over low heat, stirring, until
cheese is melted and sauce is hot.
5. Pour sauce over meat and broccoli.
6. Bake in preheated oven for 25 to 30 minutes.

BAKED MUSHROOMS MILANESE
Serves 6

1½ pounds fresh mushrooms	¼ teaspoon pepper
2 tablespoons minced parsley	¼ cup olive oil
1 clove garlic, minced	½ cup hot water
1 teaspoon dried orégano	¾ cup fresh bread crumbs
1 teaspoon salt	¼ cup grated Parmesan cheese

1. Preheat oven to 375° F. Grease small open baker (10×
6×2 inches).
2. Wash mushrooms, trim stems, and slice into baker.
3. Sprinkle with parsley, garlic, orégano, salt, pepper, and
oil. Add hot water, and sprinkle with bread crumbs and
cheese.
4. Bake in preheated oven for 25 minutes, or until crumbs
are lightly browned.

DEVILED CRAB MEAT
Serves 6

6 tablespoons butter
4 tablespoons flour
½ teaspoon salt
1 teaspoon dry mustard
½ teaspoon paprika
Pinch nutmeg
2 cups light cream

3 cups flaked cooked
Alaska king crab meat
2 tablespoons chopped
parsley
1 tablespoon lemon juice
½ cup fresh bread
crumbs

1. Preheat oven to 375° F.
2. In 2-quart saucepan melt 4 tablespoons of the butter.
Stir in flour, salt, mustard, paprika, and nutmeg. Gradually
stir in cream, and cook, stirring, until sauce is smooth
and thickened. Stir in crab meat, parsley, and lemon juice.
3. Empty mixture into small open baker (10×6×2
inches), and sprinkle with crumbs. Dot with remaining
butter.
4. Bake in preheated oven for 15 to 20 minutes, or until
crumbs are lightly brown.

CHOCOLATE-FROSTED BROWNIES
Makes 15 brownies about 2 inches square

2 ounces (2 squares)
unsweetened chocolate
½ cup butter (1 stick)
1 cup sugar
3 eggs
1 teaspoon vanilla extract

¾ cup sifted cake flour
1 teaspoon double-acting
baking powder
½ teaspoon salt
1 cup chopped or broken
walnuts

1.   Preheat oven to 325° F. Grease an open baker (10×
6×2 inches).
2.   Put chocolate and butter into a mixing bowl and set
into oven to melt. When melted, let cool slightly. Then
beat in sugar. Add eggs, one at a time, and beat well
after each addition. Stir in vanilla.
3.   Combine flour, baking powder, and salt. Stir into chocolate mixture. Stir in chopped nuts.
4.   Turn batter into baking dish and bake in preheated
oven for about 30 minutes, or until cake tester comes out
clean. Remove from oven and let cool in baking dish.
Spread top with Chocolate Glaze (see below) and cut
into serving squares.

CHOCOLATE GLAZE

In 2-quart saucepan melt 2 squares sweet chocolate (2
ounces) and 1 square bitter unsweetened chocolate (1
ounce) with 3 tablespoons butter, stirring constantly over
low heat. Remove from heat when smooth. In 10-inch
skillet heat 5 tablespoons milk. Remove from heat and stir
in 1 pound confectioners' sugar. Add sugar mixture to
chocolate mixture and beat until thick enough to spread.

PEACHES WITH COINTREAU
Serves 4

4 fresh peaches or 8	*2 tablespoons lemon juice*
peach halves canned in	*½ cup Cointreau*
light syrup	*½ cup blanched slivered*
½ cup sugar	*almonds*
¼ cup butter	

1.   Preheat oven to 375° F.

2. Peel, halve, and pit fresh peaches, or drain canned peach halves well. Arrange cut side up in open baking pan (10×6×2 inches).

3. Cream together sugar and butter. Put a heaping teaspoon of the butter mixture into center of each peach half. Sprinkle with lemon juice, Cointreau, and almonds.

4. Bake in preheated oven for 25 to 30 minutes. Serve right from baking dish.

DEEP-DISH BERRY PIE
Serves 6

4 cups fresh blueberries, blackberries, raspberries, or boysenberries	⅛ teaspoon salt
	Grated rind of ½ lemon
	1 tablespoon lemon juice
¾ cup sugar	1 tablespoon butter
1½ teaspoons tapioca or cornstarch	Pastry for a one-crust pie

1. In mixing bowl combine berries, sugar, tapioca or cornstarch, salt, lemon rind, and juice. Empty into an open baker (10×6×2 inches). Dot with butter.

2. Preheat oven to 400° F.

3. Roll pastry out on floured surface ⅛ inch thick and cut into a rectangle about 1½ inches larger than open baker. Place pastry lightly over berries and trim edges, leaving ½ inch overhanging. Moisten rim of dish, turn overhanging edge of pastry under, and press it onto rim. Flute or crimp edge of pastry with tines of a fork, and cut slits in pastry for steam to escape.

4. Bake in preheated oven for 30 to 40 minutes, or until pastry is golden.

If canned berries are used, drain well, and use only ¼ cup sugar.

SUMMER FRUIT CRUMBLE
Serves 6

3 cups diced fresh fruits (combination of banana, melon, grapes, orange segments, blueberries, and so on)
¼ cup granulated sugar
1 cup all-purpose flour
¼ teaspoon nutmeg
Dash salt
⅓ cup butter
½ cup firmly packed brown sugar
Grated rind of 1 lemon

1. Preheat oven to 375° F. Grease small open baker (10×6×2 inches).
2. Empty fruit combination into casserole and sprinkle with granulated sugar.
3. In mixing bowl combine flour, nutmeg, and salt. Cut in butter until mixture resembles coarse bread crumbs. Stir in brown sugar and lemon rind.
4 Cover fruits with the crumb mixture and bake in preheated oven for 30 minutes.
5. Serve warm in the baker with whipped cream, sour cream, or ice cream.

ORANGE CREAM CAKE
Serves 6

½ cup graham cracker
  crumbs
½ cup toasted flaked
  coconut
3 tablespoons melted
  butter
½ teaspoon vanilla
  extract

1 envelope plain gelatin
1½ cups milk
2 medium oranges
2 egg yolks
⅓ cup sugar
1 cup heavy cream,
  whipped

1. Oil a small open baker (10×6×2 inches).
2. In mixing bowl combine crumbs, coconut, melted butter, and vanilla. Spread mixture in bottom of prepared pan. Chill.
3. Soften gelatin in ½ cup of the milk in 1½-quart saucepan. Add remaining milk. Pare the thin orange skin from oranges, cut into thin strips, and add to milk. Squeeze orange juice and set aside.
4. Stir milk mixture over very low heat until gelatin is dissolved and milk is very hot.
5. In small bowl combine egg yolks, sugar, and about ½ cup of the hot milk. Gradually stir egg-sugar mixture into remaining milk in saucepan and cook over low heat, stirring constantly, for 3 minutes. Remove from heat and stir in orange juice. Cool, then chill until mixture begins to thicken, stirring occasionally.
6. Fold in whipped cream. Spoon orange cream into prepared pan, and chill until set. Cut into squares to serve.

APPLE PUDDING
Serves 6 to 8

⅓ cup all-purpose flour
1 teaspoon baking
  powder
½ teaspoon cinnamon
Dash salt
2 eggs
1½ cups sugar

1½ teaspoons vanilla
Grated rind of 1 lemon
⅔ cup chopped walnuts
8 medium tart apples,
  peeled, cored, and
  diced

1. Preheat oven to 350° F. Grease small open baker (10×6×2 inches).
2. In small mixing bowl combine flour, baking powder, cinnamon, and salt.
3. In large mixing bowl beat eggs until light. Gradually beat in sugar and continue to beat until mixture is thick and pale in color.
4. Fold in flour mixture, vanilla, and lemon rind. Stir in walnuts and apples, and spread mixture in prepared pan.
5. Bake in preheated oven for 45 minutes.
6. Cool and serve with whipped cream or ice cream.

BAKED STUFFED PEACHES
Serves 4

1-pound 13-ounce can
  cling peach halves
½ cup finely chopped
  candied lemon peel
⅓ cup finely chopped
  walnuts

⅓ cup firmly packed
  brown sugar
¼ teaspoon cinnamon
¼ cup sweet sherry

(over)

1.   Preheat oven to 375° F. Grease open baker (10×6×2 inches).

2.   Drain peaches, reserving ½ cup of the syrup. Arrange peach halves in prepared pan, cut side up.

3.   In small bowl combine lemon peel, walnuts, sugar, and cinnamon. Fill peach halves with the mixture.

4.   Combine reserved peach syrup with sherry, and spoon half of the mixture over peaches.

5.   Bake in preheated oven for 10 minutes. Spoon remaining sherry mixture over peaches and bake for 15 minutes longer.

6.   Serve plain or with vanilla ice cream.

DELECTABLE NUT BARS
Makes about 5 dozen

1¾ cups all-purpose flour
⅓ cup granulated sugar
¾ cup butter or
   margarine
¾ cup firmly packed
   brown sugar
¾ teaspoon baking
   powder

¼ teaspoon salt
3 eggs, beaten
1 teaspoon vanilla
1 cup chopped blanched
   almonds
1 cup chopped mixed
   candied peel

1.   Preheat oven to 350° F. Grease open baker (10×6×2 inches).

2.   Make cookie base: Combine 1½ cups of the flour and granulated sugar in mixing bowl. Add butter, and cut in with pastry cutter or 2 knives until mixture resembles coarse crumbs. Work mixture with hands until it forms a ball. Press dough evenly into bottom of prepared pan. Bake in preheated oven for 25 minutes.

3. Meanwhile prepare topping: In mixing bowl combine remaining ¼ cup flour with brown sugar, baking powder, and salt. Add eggs and vanilla, and beat until smooth. Stir in almonds and peel, and spread on top of baked cookie base in pan.

4. Bake in preheated oven for 30 minutes. Cool for 5 minutes, then cut into 1×2-inch bars. Remove from pan to wire rack to cool.

Large Open Baker

ROAST BEEF AND GRAVY
Serves 8

5 to 6 pounds boneless
   top sirloin of beef
Large piece of beef suet
   from butcher

2 tablespoons flour
3 cups water
1 teaspoon salt
¼ teaspoon pepper

1. Preheat oven to 425° F.

2. Place beef in large open baker (14×8½×2 inches). Place suet on top. Roast in preheated oven for 10 minutes. Reduce oven temperature to 350° F. and roast for 2 hours longer, or until beef is desired degree of doneness. A meat thermometer inserted into thickest part of roast will register:

        140° F. for rare
        160° F. for medium
        170° F. for well done

3. Transfer beef to serving platter and keep in a warm place.

4.   Remove all but about 2 tablespoons fat from roasting pan and place over direct heat. Sprinkle bottom of pan with flour, and stir, scraping in all brown bits from sides and bottom of pan.

5.   Gradually stir in water, and cook over moderate heat, stirring constantly, until gravy is smooth and thickened. Season with salt and pepper, and simmer for 5 minutes.

6.   Strain gravy into sauceboat and serve with roast beef.

STUFFED LOIN OF PORK
Serves 6

2 tablespoons butter or margarine	½ teaspoon thyme
1 medium onion, chopped	½ teaspoon basil
	⅛ teaspoon pepper
½ cup chopped celery	½ teaspoon salt
¼ cup chopped parsley	⅓ cup applesauce
2 cups fresh bread crumbs	4-pound loin of pork, cut through between bones

1.   Preheat oven to 350° F.

2.   In 10-inch skillet melt butter, and in it sauté onion and celery for 5 minutes. Remove from heat, and stir in parsley, crumbs, thyme, basil, pepper, and salt. Stir in applesauce.

3.   Spread stuffing between the chops, press roast back into shape, and tie securely with string.

4.   Place roast on rack in large open baker (14×8½×2

inches), and roast in preheated oven for 2½ hours.

5. Remove string and transfer roast to serving platter.

OVEN-FRIED CHICKEN
Serves 4

1 egg	¼ teaspoon crushed
2 tablespoons milk	rosemary
1 teaspoon Worcestershire	1¾-pound frying chicken,
sauce	cut into serving pieces
1 teaspoon dried parsley	2 cups fresh bread
flakes	crumbs
1 teaspoon salt	¼ cup butter or
¼ teaspoon pepper	margarine

1. Preheat oven to 375° F.

2. In flat dish combine egg with milk, Worcestershire, parsley, salt, pepper, and rosemary.

3. Dip chicken in egg mixture, then coat well with crumbs. Press crumbs into chicken with flat side of a knife.

4. Put butter into large open baker and set into oven until butter is melted.

5. Remove pan from oven and dip chicken into the melted butter, turning to coat both sides well.

6. Arrange chicken in pan, skin side up, and bake in preheated oven for 30 minutes. Turn chicken and continue to bake for 30 minutes longer.

BARBECUED SPARERIBS
Serves 2 for dinner; 4 for appetizer

Heavy-duty aluminum foil
2-pound slab spareribs
Monosodium glutamate
Salt and coarsely ground pepper
2 cloves garlic, minced

4 tablespoons chopped chutney
4 tablespoons soy sauce
¼ teaspoon ground ginger
3 tablespoons chili sauce
1 tablespoon honey

1. Preheat oven to 325° F. Line large open baker (14× 8½×2 inches) with sheet of foil long enough to seal over the spareribs. Place spareribs on the foil and sprinkle well with monosodium glutamate, salt, and pepper. Bring foil up and over spareribs and seal tightly with a double fold. Steam in preheated oven for 1 hour.
2. Meanwhile combine remaining ingredients.
3. Remove baker from oven. Increase oven temperature to 375° F. Open foil and roll back around spareribs. Spread ribs with the savory mixture. Bake in preheated oven for 1 hour longer, basting several times with sauce and liquid in baking pan.

HAM IN CRUMB CRUST
Serves 10

6- to 7-pound fully cooked bone in ham butt
1½ cups dry bread crumbs

2 teaspoons dry mustard
1 tablespoon paprika

1. Preheat oven to 325° F.
2. Place ham on rack in open baker (14×8½×2 inches) and bake in preheated oven for 30 minutes.
3. Remove ham from oven and cut off rind. Mark outside
4. In small bowl combine crumbs, mustard, and paprika. Press crumb mixture over ham.
5. Return ham to oven and bake for 1½ hours.

MUSTARD-GLAZED HAM
Serves 12

7- to 8-pound fully cooked bone in ham butt
3 tablespoons prepared mustard
½ cup firmly packed brown sugar

1. Preheat oven to 325° F.
2. Place ham in open baker (14×8½×2 inches) and bake in preheated oven for 2 hours.
3. Remove ham from oven and cut off skin. Mark outside fat layer with diagonal cuts to form a diamond pattern. Increase oven temperature to 450° F.
4. Meanwhile, prepare glaze: In small bowl blend mustard and sugar to form a paste.
5. Spread mustard paste oven ham.
6. Return ham to oven and bake for 25 to 30 minutes.

STUFFED LEG OF LAMB
Serves 8

2 tablespoons butter or
  margarine
⅓ cup chopped onions
⅓ cup chopped celery
¼ cup chopped green
  pepper
1 cup finely chopped
  fresh mushrooms

1 cup raw rice
2 cups beef stock or
  consommé
1 teaspoon salt
¼ teaspoon pepper
6-pound leg of lamb,
  boned

1. Preheat oven to 325° F.
2. Prepare stuffing: Melt butter or margarine in a 10-inch skillet, and in it sauté onions, celery, and green pepper for 5 minutes.
3. Add mushrooms and rice, and cook, stirring, for 2 to 3 minutes.
4. Add stock, salt, and pepper, and bring to boil. Cover skillet tightly, reduce heat to low and cook for 15 to 20 minutes, or until all liquid has been absorbed by the rice. Let cool a little.
5. Fill pocket in the lamb, where bone was removed, with the stuffing and tie roast securely with string. Place on rack in large open baker (14×8½×2 inches). Bake in preheated oven for 2½ hours, or until meat thermometer inserted into thickest part of the meat registers 175° F.
6. Transfer lamb to serving platter and remove string. Let stand in a warm place for 15 minutes before serving.

BABY LEG OF LAMB IN PASTRY
Serves 4

2 tablespoons butter or
margarine
1 small onion, finely
chopped
¼ cup finely chopped
celery
⅓ cup finely chopped
mushrooms
1 lamb kidney, finely
diced

1 egg, beaten
Salt and pepper to taste
1 baby leg of lamb
(about 2 pounds)
boned
Recipe for a one-crust
pie
1 egg yolk
1 tablespoon milk

1.   Prepare stuffing: Melt butter in 10-inch skillet and in it cook onion and celery over low heat for 5 minutes. Add mushrooms and kidney, and cook until kidney changes color, stirring frequently. Stir in beaten egg, and cook, stirring, until egg becomes firm. Remove stuffing from heat and season with salt and pepper.

2.   Fill cavity in leg of lamb with stuffing, and reshape the leg.

3.   Preheat oven to 450° F. Grease large baking dish (14× 8½×2 inches).

4.   Roll out pastry ¼ inch thick. Place lamb in center of pastry. Moisten edges of pastry and fold over lamb, sealing edges to enclose it completely. Cut off excess pastry and use to make "leaves" to decorate top of pastry. Make a slit in center of pastry and arrange "leaves" around the cut. Place in prepared pan.

5.   Combine egg yolk and milk and brush over pastry.

6.   Bake in preheated oven for 10 minutes. Reduce oven

temperature to 350° F. and continue to bake for 1 hour longer, or until pastry is golden.

7. Transfer lamb to serving platter and let stand for 10 minutes before serving. Serve with mint sauce.

ROAST RACKS OF BABY LAMB
Serves 4

2 racks of baby lamb, trimmed, about 1½ pounds each
Salt and pepper
1 tablespoon dry mustard

2 tablespoons white wine
½ cup fresh bread crumbs
2 tablespoons minced parsley

1. Preheat oven to 400° F.
2. Arrange racks of lamb in open baker (14×8½×2 inches), and sprinkle generously with salt and pepper.
3. Roast in preheated oven for 20 minutes.
4. Combine mustard and wine and brush on lamb. Mix crumbs and parsley and sprinkle over lamb.
5. Continue to roast for about 10 minutes, or until crumbs are golden.

BARBECUED RACKS OF BABY LAMB
Serves 4

½ cup barbecue sauce
1 teaspoon Worcestershire sauce
2 tablespoons minced parsley

1 teaspoon dry onion flakes
¼ teaspoon thyme
2 racks of baby lamb, about 1 pound each

1. Combine barbecue sauce, Worcestershire, parsley, onion flakes, and thyme. Spread mixture on bottom of an open baker (14×8½×2 inches).
2. Cut breasts of lamb between bones and roll in the sauce to coat each one. Let marinate in the sauce for about 12 hours in refrigerator.
3. Preheat oven to 375° F.
4. Turn ribs over in sauce and bake in preheated oven for 45 minutes.

STUFFED LEG OF VEAL
Serves 6

3½- to 4-pound boned rolled leg of veal (save bones)	Salt
	Pepper
½ cup fresh bread crumbs	1 medium onion, coarsely cut
1 teaspoon crumbled sage	1 bay leaf
1 tablespoon minced parsley	6 carrots, scraped and halved lengthwise
2 teaspoons minced garlic	3 tablespoons tomato paste
1 egg yolk	½ cup water
¼ cup heavy cream	½ cup white wine

1. Preheat oven to 400° F.
2. Untie meat and place open on flat surface.
3. Combine bread crumbs, sage, parsley, garlic, egg yolk, cream, salt, and pepper to taste, and mix well. Spread mixture in a thin layer over meat. Reshape meat and tie securely. Place seam side down in open baker (14×8½×2

inches) and sprinkle with salt and pepper. Place bones
around the roast and add onion, bay leaf, and carrots.
4. Bake in preheated oven for 30 minutes. Turn roast
seam side up and continue to bake for 30 minutes longer.
5. Combine tomato paste, water, and wine. Turn roast
again and pour tomato mixture over it. Bake for 1½ hours,
basting frequently with sauce in pan.
6. Transfer meat to a warm serving platter and garnish
with carrots. Strain sauce and serve separately.

ROAST CHICKENS
Serves 6

2 small roasting
  chickens, about 2½
  pounds each
Salt and pepper

Chicken liver stuffing
  (see Index)
3 slices bacon, halved

1. Preheat oven to 325° F.
2. Sprinkle cavities of chickens with salt and pepper, stuff
chickens with chicken liver stuffing, and truss.
3. Place chickens, breast side up, in open baker (14×8½
×2 inches) and arrange bacon slices over the breasts.
4. Bake in preheated oven for 2 hours, or until juice that
runs out of thigh muscle when tested with a fork is clear,
with no tinge of pink.
5. Untruss chickens and discard bacon. Transfer to warm
serving dish.

HERB-ROASTED CHICKEN WITH CREAM SAUCE
Serves 6

⅓ cup butter
1 clove garlic, minced
½ teaspoon dried basil
¼ teaspoon dried
  tarragon
1 tablespoon parsley
  flakes
Salt

Pepper
5-pound roasting chicken,
  trussed and ready to
  cook
3 tablespoons flour
1 chicken bouillon cube
1½ cups water
1 cup light cream

1.   Preheat oven to 350° F.
2.   In 1½-quart saucepan melt butter. Stir in garlic, basil, tarragon, parsley flakes, 1 teaspoon salt, and ¼ teaspoon pepper. Simmer over low heat for 3 minutes.
3.   Place chicken in open baker (14×8½×2 inches) and brush generously with half the butter mixture. Cover chicken lightly with aluminum foil and roast in preheated oven for 1 hour.
4.   Remove foil and brush chicken with remaining butter mixture. Roast for 45 minutes longer, basting chicken frequently with juices in pan.
5.   Remove chicken from pan to serving platter, untruss, and keep warm.
6.   Pour off all but about 3 tablespoons fat from roasting pan and place over direct heat. Stir in flour, ½ teaspoon salt and ⅛ teaspoon pepper. Add bouillon cube. Gradually stir in water and cook, stirring constantly, until sauce is smooth and thickened. Stir well from bottom and sides of pan.
7.   Stir in cream and simmer for 3 minutes. Strain sauce into a sauce boat and serve with the chicken.

DELUXE SUPPER HASH
Serves 6

2 pounds potatoes
2 tablespoons butter or
  margarine
1 medium onion,
  chopped
2 1-pound cans
  corned-beef hash
¼ cup chopped parsley
1 teaspoon Worcestershire
  sauce

½ cup milk
Salt and pepper to taste
6 eggs
½ cup fresh bread
  crumbs
¼ cup grated Parmesan
  cheese

1.   Peel and slice potatoes. Cook in boiling salted water to cover for 10 minutes, or until fork tender.
2.   Preheat oven to 350° F. Grease large open baker (14× 8½×2 inches).
3.   Drain potatoes and spread in bottom of prepared pan.
4.   In 10-inch skillet melt butter, and in it sauté onion until transparent. Stir in hash, parsley, Worcestershire, and milk. Season with salt and pepper.
5.   Spread hash mixture over potatoes in pan and make six indentations over surface with back of a large spoon. Drop an egg into each indentation.
6.   Sprinkle with crumbs mixed with cheese.
7.   Bake in preheated oven for 20 minutes. Turn on broiler heat and broil for 5 minutes to brown surface.

LASAGNE

Serves 6 to 8

1 *pound wide lasagne*
noodles
Spaghetti sauce (see
Index)
1 *pound Ricotta cheese*

1 *pound Mozzarella*
cheese, thinly sliced
½ *cup grated Parmesan*
cheese

1. In 3-quart saucepan cook noodles in boiling salted water according to package directions. Drain well and cover with cold water.
2. Preheat oven to 350° F. Grease large open baker (14× 8½×2 inches).
3. Drain about ¼ of the noodles and arrange on bottom of baker. Cover with a layer of spaghetti sauce and dot with Ricotta cheese, using about ¼ of it. Cover with ¼ of the Mozzarella cheese and sprinkle with 2 tablespoons Parmesan.
4. Repeat layers, finishing with the cheeses.
5. Bake in preheated oven for 45 minutes. Serve right in the baking dish.

APPLESAUCE CAKE WITH LEMON FROSTING

1½ cup light raisins
½ cup shortening
1½ cups light brown
   sugar, firmly packed
2 eggs
1½ cups thick
   unsweetened applesauce
3 cups sifted cake flour
1½ teaspoons baking
   soda

¾ teaspoon salt
1 teaspoon ground
   cinnamon
1 teaspoon ground
   nutmeg
½ teaspoon ground
   cloves
1 cup broken nut meats

1. Cover raisins with boiling water and set aside for 10 minutes for raisins to plump.
2. Preheat oven to 300° F. Grease a large open baker (14×8½×2 inches).
3. In large mixing bowl cream shortening. Gradually beat in sugar. Add eggs, one at a time, beating well after each addition. Stir in applesauce.
4. Combine flour, baking soda, salt, and spices. Stir into applesauce mixture.
5. Drain raisins well, and stir raisins and nuts into batter.
6. Pour batter into open baker and bake in preheated oven for 1¼ hours, or until cake tester inserted in center comes out clean.
7. Let cool in open baker and, when cool, frost with Lemon Frosting (see page 153).

LEMON FROSTING

⅓ cup butter	2 tablespoons lemon
Grated rind of 1 lemon	juice
3 cups confectioners'	About 1 tablespoon
sugar (sift if lumpy)	water

1. In mixing bowl cream butter with lemon rind until fluffy. Stir in ¼ cup of the confectioners' sugar. Stir in lemon juice.
2. Gradually stir in remaining confectioners' sugar, adding a few drops of water as needed, to make an icing with a creamy spreading consistency.

PARTY PINEAPPLE FREEZE
Serves 8 to 10

12 macaroons, crumbled	⅓ cup sugar
13½-ounce can crushed	2 eggs, separated
pineapple	1 teaspoon rum flavoring
1 envelope plain	1 cup heavy cream,
gelatin	whipped

1. Oil a large open baker (14×8½×2 inches). Sprinkle bottom with macaroon crumbs. Set aside.
2. Drain pineapple juice into 2-quart saucepan. Add gelatin and let soften, then stir over low heat until juice is hot and gelatin is completely dissolved. Cool.
3. In mixing bowl beat sugar and egg yolks until mixture is light and fluffy. Stir in cooled gelatin and rum flavoring.
4. Beat egg whites until stiff but not dry and fold into

egg-sugar mixture. Fold in crushed pineapple and whipped cream.

5. Pour into prepared pan and cover with foil.

6. Freeze until firm.

7. About 1 hour before serving, unmold onto serving dish and transfer to refrigerator until ready to serve.

Open Roasting or Paella Pan

Here are just a few basic roasts for your largest roaster. Actually a large open roaster may be used for any large roasting recipes in your general cookbooks or for large quantity party or buffet dishes where it is advantageous to use oven-to-table cookware.

ROAST TURKEY
Serves 16 to 20

18- to 20-pound
   ready-to-cook turkey
Salt and pepper
Sausage stuffing (see
   Index)

½ cup melted butter or
   margarine
Giblet gravy (see
   Index)

1. Preheat oven to 325° F. Grease a large open roasting pan.

2. Sprinkle neck and body cavity of the turkey with salt and pepper.

3. Spoon sausage stuffing into cavities and fasten with poultry skewers. Truss turkey and place breast side up in large roasting pan.

4. Brush turkey skin with melted butter or margarine and cover turkey with large sheet of heavy-duty aluminum foil, folding foil under edges of pan.

5. Roast in preheated oven for 4½ hours, basting occasionally with drippings in pan. Remove foil and roast for 30 minutes longer, or until meat thermometer registers 190° F., basting every 10 minutes.

6. Remove trussing and skewers, and let turkey stand in a warm place for 30 minutes before carving. Serve with giblet gravy.

RIB ROAST WITH YORKSHIRE PUDDING
Serves 8

4-rib standing roast beef (about 12 pounds)	¼ teaspoon salt
	1 cup milk
1 cup flour	2 eggs

1. Preheat oven to 325° F.

2. Arrange roast on bone ends in large open roaster or paella pan. Bake in preheated oven for 4 hours, or until done to taste.

3. Meanwhile prepare pudding batter: In mixing bowl combine flour and salt. Add ½ cup of the milk and eggs and beat with rotary beater or on medium speed until batter is smooth. Add remaining milk and beat until surface of liquid is covered with air bubbles. Let stand for 30 minutes.

4. Remove beef from pan to serving platter and keep warm. Turn oven heat up to 425° F.

5. Drain all but about ¼ cup beef drippings from roaster and return roaster to oven for 5 minutes.

6.   Pour batter into hot roasting pan and bake in the hot oven for 25 minutes, or until pudding is puffed and well browned.

7.   Cut pudding into serving pieces and serve with the roast.

BONED LAMB ROAST
Serves 6 to 8

6-pound leg of lamb, boned	2 teaspoons salt
1 cup commercial sour cream	½ teaspoon pepper
4 shallots or green onions, minced	⅓ cup grated Parmesan cheese
¼ cup chopped parsley	2 teaspoons good curry powder

1.   Preheat oven to 325° F.

2.   Trim excess fat from leg of lamb and spread out flat.

3.   Combine remaining ingredients and spread half of the mixture over inside of lamb. Roll leg and secure with string.

4.   Place lamb in open roaster and spread with remaining sour-cream mixture.

5.   Roast in preheated oven for 2½ to 3 hours, or until lamb is done to taste.

Large Stove-to-Table
3½-Quart Open Baker or Paella Dish

PARTY TETRAZZINI
Serves 8 to 10

½ cup butter
1 pound mushrooms,
  sliced
⅓ cup flour
3½ cups chicken broth
1 cup heavy cream
¼ cup sherry
1 teaspoon monosodium
  glutamate

1½ teaspoons salt or to
  taste
1 cup grated Parmesan
  cheese
1 pound spaghetti,
  cooked and drained
5 cups cooked diced
  chicken or turkey or
  flaked crab meat

1. In 2-quart saucepan melt butter and in it sauté mushrooms for 5 minutes. Stir in flour. Gradually stir in chicken broth, and cook, stirring, until sauce is thickened. Stir in cream, sherry, monosodium glutamate, salt, and half the cheese. Simmer for 5 minutes, stirring frequently.
2. Preheat oven to 375° F. Butter an attractive open baker or paella dish.
3. Arrange one third of the spaghetti in the dish, sprinkle with half the chicken, turkey, or crab meat and top with one third of the sauce. Repeat with another layer of spaghetti, remaining chicken, turkey, or crab meat, and half the remaining sauce. Cover with remaining spaghetti and rest of sauce. Sprinkle with remaining cheese.
4. Bake in preheated oven for 35 to 40 minutes. Take from stove to table.

QUICK MEXICAN DINNER
Serves 10 to 12

½ cup olive or cooking
  oil
2 large onions, chopped
4 15-ounce cans tamales
  in chili gravy
2 15-ounce cans chili con
  carne without beans

3 15-ounce cans chili con
  carne with beans
1 teaspoon orégano
2 cups shredded Cheddar
  or Monterey Jack
  cheese

1. In attractive 3½-quart open baker or paella dish heat
oil over direct heat and in it braise onions for 10 minutes,
or until they are tender.
2. Preheat oven to 350° F.
3. Unwrap tamales and arrange half in a layer over onions
in dish.
4. Add chili con carne with and without beans, sprinkle
with orégano, and top with a layer of the remaining
tamales.
5. Bake in preheated oven for 30 minutes, or until bubbling hot.
6. Sprinkle with cheese and bake for 15 minutes longer,
or until cheese is melted. Take directly to table.

ARROZ CON POLLO (Chicken with Rice)
Serves 8

½ cup olive oil
8 serving pieces chicken
3 teaspoons salt
½ teaspoon pepper
1 teaspoon orégano
1 bay leaf
1 medium onion,
  chopped
2 cloves garlic, minced
3 tomatoes, fresh or
  canned, chopped

2 cups raw rice
½ teaspoon saffron
1 cup dry white wine
5 cups chicken broth
3½ ounces split
  blanched almonds
5 tablespoons butter
12 medium mushrooms
  (1 pound) quartered
Pimiento and parsley for
  garnish

1. Preheat oven to 325° F.
2. In attractive 3½-quart open baker or paella dish heat olive oil. Place chicken pieces in the hot oil and sauté until lightly browned on one side. Turn chicken pieces, sprinkle with salt, pepper, and orégano. Add bay leaf. Transfer dish to preheated oven, and bake for 15 minutes.
3. Sprinkle chicken with onion, and bake for 45 minutes longer.
4. Add garlic, tomatoes, and rice, and mix well. Add saffron, wine, and 3 cups chicken broth. Bake for 45 minutes.
5. Meanwhile sauté almonds until golden and crisp in 1 tablespoon butter in a 10-inch skillet. Set aside. Sauté mushrooms in same skillet in remaining butter for 5 minutes. Set aside.
6. Add remaining chicken broth to rice and chicken,

sprinkle with almonds and mushrooms, and return to oven for 15 minutes.

7. Serve in the baking dish, garnished with strips of pimiento and clusters of parsley.

Individual Baking or Au Gratin Dishes

Small, shallow baking dishes, round or oval, each designed to hold from one to two cups of food for individual service, are a welcome addition to kitchen and table cookware. Dozens of different dishes may be quickly cooked in these versatile small bakers, running the gamut from the popular baked or broiled scampito breakfast eggs *au plat*, eggs Benedict or Florentine, creamed fish or shellfish, stuffed vegetables, veal scallops Marsala, and many pasta dishes.

Almost any recipe in this chapter for small or large baking dishes may be divided and baked and cooked and served in individual baking dishes. Recipes that serve four, would be divided into four individual dishes; recipes that serve six would be divided into six. Baking time would be reduced accordingly, or from 10 to 15 minutes less baking for most dishes.

SCAMPI

Count on at least 1 pound of shrimp to serve 3
Per serving:

6 *very large or 8 to 10*
medium shrimp
1 *tablespoon butter*
1 *tablespoon olive oil*
Pinch *dried basil*
1 *tablespoon chopped*
parsley

1 *teaspoon lemon juice*
1 *clove garlic, minced*
¼ *teaspoon salt*
Freshly *ground black*
pepper

1.   Peel and devein shrimp, leaving tails attached. Split body of each shrimp lengthwise down the back, being careful not to cut all the way through. Spread shrimp out butterfly-fashion.
2.   Preheat oven to 450° F.
3.   In a flameproof, ovenproof au gratin dish, heat butter until melted and foamy over moderate heat. Remove from heat and stir in olive oil, basil, parsley, lemon juice, garlic, salt, and lots of freshly ground pepper.
4.   Arrange shrimp in the dish, turning each to coat thoroughly with the savory butter.
5.   Bake in preheated oven for 6 minutes for medium shrimp; 8 minutes for large. Serve hot from the oven with hot Italian bread to dip in the sauce.

NOTE: Scampi may be broiled, but are much better cooked in a hot oven.

EGGS SUR LE PLAT

For each serving:

2 *slices bacon or 2 link sausages*
2 *eggs*
Salt

1. Preheat oven to 350° F.
2. Sauté bacon or sausages in skillet until brown. Drain on absorbent paper.
3. Pour 1 tablespoon of the bacon or sausage fat into an individual flameproof, ovenproof au gratin dish. Break eggs into the hot fat.
4. Cook over low heat for 1 minute, then tip dish enough to be able to spoon a little of the hot fat over the yolks. Sprinkle with a little salt.
5. Transfer dish to preheated oven and cook for 10 minutes, or until eggs are done to taste. Garnish with bacon or sausages before serving.

HAM 'N' EGGS DELUXE

Serves 4

2 *tablespoons butter or margarine*
1 *small onion, finely chopped*
1 *cup finely chopped mushrooms*
2 *cups ground cooked ham*
1 *tablespoon tomato paste*

2 *tablespoons chopped parsley*
¼ *teaspoon prepared mustard*
2 *tablespoons water*
Salt and pepper
4 *eggs*
¼ *cup light cream*
½ *cup grated Cheddar cheese*

1. Preheat oven to 375° F. Grease 4 individual au gratin dishes.
2. In 10-inch skillet melt butter or margarine, and in it sauté onion for 5 minutes. Add mushrooms and ham, and sauté for 5 minutes.
3. Stir in tomato paste, parsley, mustard, and water. Season lightly with salt and pepper.
4. Press ham mixture on bottom of prepared dishes, dividing evenly, and make an indentation in center of each with back of a spoon.
5. Break an egg into center of each dish and sprinkle with cream and cheese.
6. Bake in preheated oven for 20 minutes, or until eggs are set to taste.

CRAB AU GRATIN
Serves 4

2 tablespoons butter	Dash Tabasco
1 small onion, finely chopped	Salt and pepper
2 tablespoons flour	4 large slices of tomato
1 cup milk	2 6-ounce packages frozen cooked Alaska
1 cup grated Cheddar cheese	crab meat, thawed
¼ teaspoon dry mustard	¼ cup dry bread crumbs

1. Preheat oven to 400° F. Grease 4 individual au gratin dishes.
2. In 1½-quart saucepan melt butter, and in it sauté onion for 5 minutes. Stir in flour. Gradually stir in milk,

and cook, stirring constantly, until sauce is smooth and thickened.

3. Remove from heat and stir in cheese, mustard, and Tabasco. Season with salt and pepper.

4. Arrange tomato slice in bottom of each dish. Top with lumps of crab meat. Pour sauce over crab, and sprinkle with crumbs.

5. Bake in preheated oven for 15 minutes, or until golden and bubbly.

CLAM APPETIZER
Serves 4

4 slices white bread, finely crumbed
6 tablespoons butter
3 tablespoons flour
Pinch dried tarragon

9-ounce can minced clams
1½ cups mixed clam liquid and milk
1 egg

1. In 10-inch skillet melt 3 tablespoons of the butter and in it sauté bread crumbs until golden. Set aside.

2. In 1½-quart saucepan melt remaining 3 tablespoons butter. Stir in flour and tarragon.

3. Drain clam liquid into measuring cup and add enough milk to make a total of 1½ cups liquid. Stir gradually into butter-flour mixture, and cook, stirring constantly, until sauce is smooth and thickened. Remove from heat.

4. Beat egg lightly in cup or small bowl and stir in ½ cup of the hot sauce. Stir egg mixture gradually into sauce in pan. Cool slightly, then stir in clams.

5. Preheat oven to 350° F. while sauce is cooking.

6. Sprinkle a little crumb mixture into bottom of each

gratin dish. Divide clam mixture into dishes and sprinkle top with remaining crumbs.

7. Bake in preheated oven for 15 minutes, or until sauce is bubbling. Serve hot.

SHRIMPS AU GRATIN
Serves 4

1 cup dry white wine
1 small bay leaf
1 stalk celery, diced
1 teaspoon salt
¼ teaspoon peppercorns
2 pound shrimp, shelled
   and deveined
6 tablespoons butter
3 small shallots or
   green onions, finely
   chopped

2 tablespoons finely
   chopped green pepper
2 tablespoons flour
1 cup heavy cream
2 egg yolks
2 tablespoons finely
   chopped parsley
½ cup fresh bread
   crumbs
¼ cup grated Parmesan
   cheese

1. Preheat oven to 375° F. Butter 4 individual au gratin dishes.

2. In 2-quart saucepan combine wine, bay leaf, celery, salt, and peppercorns. Bring to a boil and add shrimp. Cover, and cook over very low heat for 10 minutes. Drain shrimp, reserving liquid. Strain liquid and return to saucepan. Boil over high heat until liquid is reduced to ½ cup; set aside.

3. Divide shrimp into prepared dishes.

4. In 2-quart saucepan melt 3 tablespoons of the butter. Add shallots and green pepper, and cook over low heat for 5 minutes.

5. Sprinkle vegetables with flour. Gradually stir in the ½ cup reserved liquid, and cook, stirring constantly, until sauce is thick.

6. Combine cream and egg yolks, and stir into sauce. Remove from heat.

7. Correct seasoning of sauce to taste and pour over the shrimp, dividing equally.

8. Melt remaining 3 tablespoons butter and mix with parsley, crumbs and cheese. Sprinkle over top of sauce.

9. Bake in preheated oven for 15 minutes, or until crumbs are golden and sauce is bubbling.

SCALLOPS AU GRATIN

Substitute washed scallops for shrimp in recipe above. Let cook in the seasoned liquid for 3 minutes only. If large sea scallops are used, slice in half or thirds.

LOBSTER SUPPER
Serves 2

¼ cup butter
3 shallots or green
   onions, finely chopped
1 cup finely chopped
   mushrooms
6¾-ounce can lobster,
   drained and flaked

2 tablespoons chopped
   parsley
½ cup heavy cream
Dash Tabasco
Salt and pepper
2 eggs

1. Preheat oven to 350° F. Grease 2 individual au gratin dishes.

2. In 10-inch skillet melt butter and in it cook shallots

for 5 minutes. Stir in mushrooms, and cook for 5 minutes longer, stirring occasionally.

3. Stir in lobster, parsley, cream, and Tabasco. Season with salt and pepper to taste.

4. Bring liquid to a simmer, then remove from heat and divide into prepared dishes.

5. Break an egg into center of each and bake in preheated oven for 20 minutes, or until eggs are set to taste.

BEEF COBBLER

Serves 4

1 tablespoon shortening
1 medium onion, chopped
1 pound ground beef
2 8-ounce cans tomato sauce
2 tablespoons instant oats
2 tablespoons chopped parsley
½ teaspoon dried basil
Salt and pepper to taste

¾ cup flour
½ teaspoon salt
1 teaspoon baking powder
¼ teaspoon dry mustard
1 tablespoon butter
½ cup grated Cheddar cheese
1 egg
½ cup milk

1. Preheat oven to 425° F. Grease 4 individual au gratin dishes.

2. In 10-inch skillet melt shortening, and in it sauté onion and beef until meat loses all red color.

3. Stir in tomato sauce, oats, parsley, basil, and salt and pepper. Simmer over low heat for 15 minutes.

4. Meanwhile prepare topping: In mixing bowl combine

flour, salt, baking powder, and mustard. Cut in butter until mixture resembles fine crumbs. Stir in cheese. Add egg and milk, and beat just until mixture is smooth.
5.   Divide beef mixture into prepared dishes. Drop batter into center of meat in each dish, dividing equally.
6.   Bake in preheated oven for 15 minutes, or until topping is golden.

VEAL PARMIGIANA
Serves 4

8 small slices leg of
    veal (about 1 pound)
    pounded thin
1 egg, beaten with 2
    tablespoons milk
¾ teaspoon salt
⅛ teaspoon pepper
2 cups fresh bread
    crumbs

¼ cup olive oil
12-ounce jar meatless
    marinara sauce
8 ounces Mozzarella
    cheese, thinly sliced
½ cup grated Parmesan
    cheese

1.   Flatten veal well by placing between pieces of wax paper and pounding with rolling pin.
2.   Beat egg mixture with salt and pepper.
3.   Dip veal slices into egg mixture, then roll in crumbs. Press crumbs into meat gently with blade of knife.
4.   In 12-inch skillet heat half the oil, and in it sauté half the veal until golden on both sides. Repeat with remaining oil and veal.
5.   Preheat oven to 375° F.
6.   Arrange 2 pieces of veal in each au gratin dish. Spoon

over half the marinara sauce. Top with Mozzarella cheese, and spoon over remaining sauce.

7. Sprinkle with Parmesan cheese and bake in preheated oven for 20 minutes.

LITTLE CHICKEN SOUFFLES
Serves 4

5 tablespoons butter	1 teaspoon lemon juice
3 chicken livers	1 teaspoon salt
1 small onion, chopped	¼ teaspoon pepper
1 cup diced cooked	Dash nutmeg
chicken	4 egg yolks
3 tablespoons flour	5 egg whites
¾ cup milk	

1. In 2-quart saucepan melt 2 tablespoons butter and in it sauté chicken livers and onion for 10 minutes. Put mixture and diced cooked chicken through medium blade of food chopper and set aside.

2. Rinse saucepan, and in it melt remaining 3 tablespoons butter. Stir in flour. Gradually stir in milk, and cook, stirring constantly, until sauce is smooth and thickened. Stir in chicken mixture, lemon juice, salt, pepper, and nutmeg, and bring to a boil. Remove from heat and beat in egg yolks. Set aside to cool a little.

3. Preheat oven to 350° F.

4   Beat egg whites until stiff, but not dry, and fold into chicken mixture. Divide into 4 individual au gratin dishes.

5. Bake in preheated oven for 30 minutes, or until puffed and golden. Serve at once.

SOLE AMANDINE
Serves 4

*4 fillets of sole (about
1½ pounds)
Salt and pepper
Juice of 1 lemon*

*½ cup butter
½ cup slivered blanched
almonds*

1.   Preheat oven to 375° F. Butter 4 individual au gratin dishes.
2.   Cut each fillet of sole in half and arrange 2 halves in bottom of each prepared dish. Sprinkle with salt, pepper, and lemon juice.
3.   Bake in preheated oven for 15 minutes. Turn oven heat to broil.
4.   Drain off excess liquids in dishes.
5.   Top sole with dots of butter, and sprinkle with almonds.
6.   Broil for 4 minutes, or until nuts are golden.

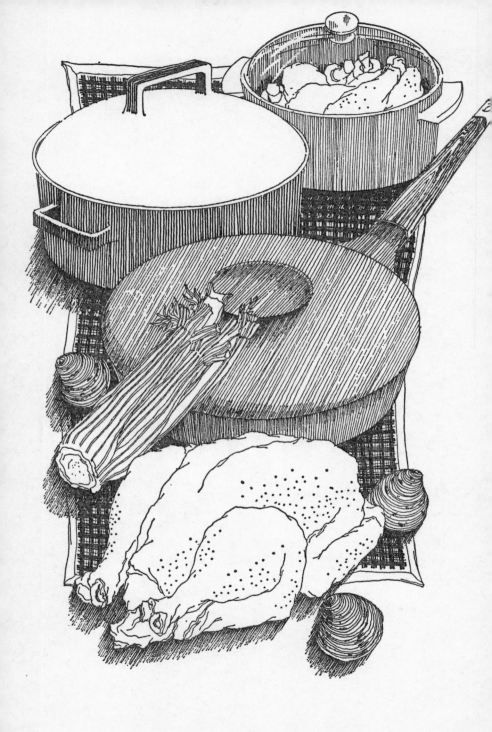

4

THE CHICKEN FRYER

Next in importance in a well-equipped kitchen, which yours is rapidly becoming, is a chicken fryer. This is a shallow-type casserole, deeper than the average baking dish or skillet, but with a high cover that gives you an over-all depth from top to bottom of about 4 inches. It is usually 11 or 12 inches in diameter, with a liquid capacity of about 4 quarts, and serves equally well for cooking on top of the stove or in the oven.

Designed primarily for cooking chicken parts or portions with the bones, it is also an excellent "Dutch oven" for braising roasts of meat and whole poultry, and makes a fine and safe deep-fat fryer.

The chicken fryer bridges the culinary gap between your largest saucepan and larger-capacity casseroles, which you may or may not need to complete your basic kitchen cookware. It is another skillet, a very large saucepan, a baking dish, a Dutch oven and a casserole all rolled in one. It's one of the best investments a good cook can make.

POULET NIVERNAIS
Serves 4

3 teaspoons salt
½ teaspoon pepper
3-pound frying chicken,
    cut into serving pieces
¼ cup butter
12 small white onions
12 mushroom caps
3 carrots, sliced
1¼ cups dry white wine
2 cloves
1 clove garlic

1 bay leaf
½ teaspoon thyme
½ teaspoon marjoram
4 sprigs parsley
½ teaspoon saffron
2 tablespoons hot water
1½ cups commercial
    sour cream
Dumpling batter (see
    below)

1.   Preheat oven to 375° F.
2.   Rub salt and pepper into chicken pieces. In chicken fryer melt butter, and in it brown chicken on all sides. Add onions, mushrooms, carrots, wine, cloves, garlic, bay leaf, thyme, marjoram, and parsley. Cover and bake in preheated oven for 1 hour.
3.   Remove chicken fryer from oven and place over direct heat.
4.   In small bowl soak saffron in hot water, then stir into chicken. Carefully stir sour cream into liquid in chicken fryer and bring just to the simmering point.
5.   Drop dumpling batter by spoonfuls into the simmering liquid. Cover and cook over low heat for 15 minutes. Serve in the chicken fryer.

DUMPLINGS

1 cup all-purpose flour
½ teaspoon salt
1½ teaspoons double-
   acting baking powder

1 tablespoon shortening
½ cup milk

1. In small mixing bowl combine flour, salt, and baking powder.
2. Work in shortening until it forms fine crumbs in the flour mixture. A pastry blender makes this easy, or use tines of a fork.
3. Add milk all at once. Mix with fork just enough to blend.

CHICKEN CACCIATORE
Serves 4

¼ cup flour
2 teaspoons salt
⅛ teaspoon pepper
1 frying chicken (about
   4 pounds), cut into
   serving pieces
¼ cup olive oil
1-pound can tomatoes
   with liquid

6-ounce can tomato
   paste
1 clove garlic, minced
8 small white onions
1 teaspoon sugar
1 bay leaf
¼ pound fresh
   mushrooms, sliced

1. In paper bag mix flour with 1 teaspoon salt and the pepper. Add chicken and shake well to coat the pieces lightly.
2. Heat oil in chicken fryer and in it brown chicken well.

Remove chicken from pan and pour out excess oil. Add tomatoes, tomato paste, garlic, onions, sugar, and bay leaf and mix well. Bring to a boil.

3. Return chicken to pan. Cover and cook over low heat for 45 minutes.

4. Add mushrooms, cover, and simmer for 15 minutes longer, or until chicken is tender.

CHICKEN FRICASSEE WITH DUMPLINGS
Serves 8

2 *frying chickens (about 2½ pounds each), quartered*
½ *cup flour*
Salt and pepper
2 *tablespoons cooking oil*
½ *cup sliced onions*
½ *cup chopped celery with leaves*

2 *cups chicken broth*
2 *cups water*
⅓ *cup flour*
1 *cup light cream*
Salt and pepper to taste
Drop egg dumpling batter (see below)

1. Coat chicken pieces with the ½ cup flour mixed with 1½ teaspoon salt and ¼ teaspoon pepper.

2. Heat oil in chicken fryer, brown chicken until golden on all sides. Add onions, celery, chicken broth, and water. Cover and simmer for 45 minutes, or until chicken is tender.

3. Remove chicken and keep warm. Remove excess fat from surface of liquid, and add water or chicken broth to make a total of 4 cups liquid. Bring liquid to a simmer.

4. Combine the flour and cream. Stir into broth, and cook, stirring constantly, until sauce is smooth and thickened. Correct seasoning with salt and pepper.

5. Replace chicken in sauce and drop egg dumpling batter

by spoonfuls into the simmering gravy. Cook, uncovered, for 10 minutes. Cover and cook for 10 minutes longer. Serve right from the chicken fryer.

DROP EGG DUMPLINGS

2 cups all-purpose flour
1 teaspoon salt
3 tablespoons baking
  powder

1 egg
¾ cup milk
2 tablespoons melted
  butter

1. While chicken is simmering, combine flour, salt, and baking powder on piece of wax paper.
2. In mixing bowl beat egg with milk. Stir in flour mixture. Stir in melted butter.

BRUNSWICK STEW
Serves 6

4-pound roasting
  chicken, cut into
  serving pieces
½ cup flour
2 teaspoons salt
¼ teaspoon cayenne
4 tablespoons butter
4 tablespoons cooking
  oil
½ cup chopped onions

2½ cups stewed
  tomatoes
1 teaspoon Worcestershire
  sauce
1 teaspoon sugar
Salt and pepper to taste
1-pound can whole
  kernel corn, drained
10-ounce package frozen
  Lima beans

1. Put chicken pieces in paper bag with flour, salt, and

cayenne, and shake bag to coat chicken evenly.

2. In chicken fryer heat butter and oil and in it brown chicken pieces lightly on all sides. Add onions, and cook until they are transparent.

3. Add tomatoes, Worcestershire sauce, sugar, and salt and pepper to taste. Cover and cook over low heat for 1½ hours, or until chicken is tender.

4. Add corn and beans, cover and cook for 20 minutes longer. Serve with corn bread.

SAUTEED CHICKEN
Serves 6

½ cup flour
2 teaspoons salt
¼ teaspoon pepper
2 chickens, about 3
  pounds each, cut into
  serving portions or 6
  serving pieces of
  chicken

¼ cup cooking oil
¼ cup butter

1. In paper bag combine flour, salt, and pepper. Add chicken pieces, a few at a time, and shake to coat chicken evenly with flour mixture.

2. In chicken fryer heat oil and butter over moderate heat. Arrange chicken pieces in the hot fat, and cook for about 20 minutes, or until lightly browned on all sides, turning frequently with tongs.

3. Reduce heat to low, cover chicken, and cook for about 30 minutes, or until chicken is tender and the juice which

runs out of the thigh when pricked with a fork is clear, with no tinge of pink. For crisp chicken, uncover during last 10 minutes of cooking.

CREAM GRAVY

Remove chicken from skillet to warm serving platter and keep warm. To juices remaining in pan add 3 tablespoons butter. When butter is melted stir in 3 tablespoons flour, ½ teaspoon salt and some freshly ground pepper. Stir over moderate heat until mixture bubbles. Gradually stir in 1 cup warm milk and cook, stirring in all brown bits from bottom and sides of fryer, until gravy is smooth and thick. Stir in ½ cup cream. Pour gravy over chicken and sprinkle with paprika or chopped parsley.

SAUTEED CHICKEN WITH VEGETABLES

Follow recipe for Sautéed Chicken. When chicken is brown, add to chicken fryer 1 medium onion, finely chopped, 1 green pepper, seeded and chopped, and 1 cup sliced mushrooms, canned or fresh. Cover and cook for about 30 minutes, or until chicken is tender. Remove to warm serving platter and sprinkle with chopped parsley.

CHICKEN PAPRIKASH

Follow recipe for Sautéed Chicken. When chicken is brown, add 1 medium onion, finely chopped, 1 tablespoon paprika and ½ cup chicken broth or dry white wine. Turn chicken so that all pieces are flavored with paprika. Cover and cook for about 30 minutes, or until chicken is tender. Arrange chicken on warm serving platter. Into juices in pan stir 1 cup warm cream, sweet or sour, and cook, stirring, until sauce is hot. Pour over chicken.

CHICKEN CACCIATORE WITH WHITE WINE

Follow recipe for Sautéed Chicken. When chicken is brown, add 2 medium onions, sliced, 1 cup sliced fresh mushrooms, 1 green pepper, seeded and sliced, 1 clove garlic, minced, 1 cup canned tomatoes, ½ cup dry white wine, ¼ teaspoon dried tarragon, 1 bay leaf and 2 tablespoons chopped parsley. Cover and cook for 30 minutes, or until chicken is tender.

CHICKEN CACCIATORE WITH RED WINE

Follow recipe for Sautéed Chicken. When chicken is brown add 3 cloves garlic, minced, 2 cups chopped onion, 1 green pepper, seeded and chopped, ½ teaspoon dried sweet basil or tarragon, 1 cup stewed tomatoes and ½ cup dry red wine. Cover and cook over low heat for 30 minutes, or until chicken is tender.

CHICKEN CANTONESE

Follow recipe for Sautéed Chicken. When chicken is brown add 2 cloves garlic, minced and 1 cup chicken broth. Cover and cook over low heat for 30 minutes, or until chicken is tender. Remove chicken and keep warm. To juices in pan add ¼ cup ginger syrup, ¼ cup chopped preserved ginger, and 1 tablespoon lemon juice. Bring sauce to a boil. Stir in 1 tablespoon cornstarch mixed with 3 tablespoons cold water, and cook, stirring, until sauce is thickened. Return chicken to fryer and sprinkle with 2 tablespoons chopped parsley. Cook for 5 minutes. Serve with cooked rice (see Index).

CHICKEN BREASTS SMOTHERED IN RICE
Serves 6

¼ cup butter
3 whole chicken breasts, cut in half and skinned
1 medium onion, finely chopped
½ cup chopped green pepper
½ cup chopped celery

1 cup chopped mushrooms
1¼ cups raw rice
3 cups chicken broth
2 teaspoons salt
¼ teaspoon pepper
½ teaspoon dried rosemary

1. In chicken fryer melt butter, and in it sauté chicken breasts until golden on both sides. Remove chicken and set aside.
2. To butter remaining in fryer add onion, green pepper, and celery, and sauté for 5 minutes. Stir in mushrooms and rice, and cook until rice is lightly brown, stirring occasionally.
3. Add broth, salt, pepper, and rosemary, and bring to a boil.
4. Replace chicken breasts in fryer, cover, and cook over low heat for 30 minutes, or until chicken is tender and all liquid has been absorbed.

CHICKEN MARENGO
Serves 4

⅓ cup flour
1½ teaspoons salt
¼ teaspoon pepper
½ teaspoon rosemary
¼ teaspoon tarragon
3-pound frying chicken,
   cut into serving pieces
¼ cup butter
1 large onion, sliced

2 cloves garlic, minced
¼ pound fresh
   mushrooms, sliced
4 large peeled tomatoes,
   fresh or canned and
   quartered
⅓ cup dry white wine
⅓ cup chopped parsley

1.   On a piece of wax paper mix flour, salt, pepper, rosemary, and tarragon.
2.   Coat chicken in the seasoned flour, reserving remaining flour mixture.
3.   In chicken fryer melt butter, and in it sauté chicken until brown on all sides. Remove chicken from pan and set aside.
4.   To fat remaining in pan add onion and garlic, and sauté over low heat for 5 minutes. Add mushroom slices, and sauté for 3 minutes longer.
5.   Sprinkle vegetables with reserved flour mixture and stir in tomatoes, wine, and parsley. Cook over low heat, stirring constantly, until sauce is thickened and simmering.
6.   Replace chicken, cover, and simmer over low heat for 40 minutes, or until chicken is tender, stirring occasionally. Serve in the chicken fryer.

COQ AU VIN
Serves 4

¼ pound bacon, diced
2½- to 3-pound chicken,
 cut into serving pieces
¼ cup brandy
Salt and pepper
2 cups red wine
10½-ounce can chicken
 broth
1 tablespoon tomato
 paste
1 small bay leaf
1 clove garlic, minced
3 tablespoons flour
¼ cup butter
1 pound small white
 onions
½ pound mushrooms

1. Sauté bacon in chicken fryer until crisp. Drain bacon and set aside. Pour off all but about 3 tablespoons fat from fryer, and in it sauté chicken pieces until browned on all sides. Sprinkle chicken with brandy, and ignite. Let flame burn out.
2. Sprinkle chicken with a little salt and pepper and the crisp bacon. Add wine, chicken broth, tomato paste, bay leaf, and garlic, and bring to a boil.
3. Combine flour with 2 tablespoons butter. Stir butter-flour mixture into liquid in chicken fryer bit by bit, and cook, stirring, until liquid is slightly thickened. Remove from heat.
4. Preheat oven to 325° F.
5. In 10-inch skillet sauté onions in 1 tablespoon butter until browned on all sides, shaking pan frequently. Arrange onions around chicken.
6. Add remaining tablespoon butter to skillet and in it sauté mushrooms for 5 minutes. Arrange mushrooms around chicken.

7. Cover and bake in preheated oven for 1 hour. Discard bay leaf before serving. Serve right in the chicken fryer.

CHICKEN SPAGHETTI
Serves 8

3- to 4-pound chicken
1 stalk celery, quartered
1 medium onion, quartered
1 carrot, quartered
Few sprigs parsley
1 bay leaf
Pinch of thyme
1 pound spaghetti
¼ cup olive oil
½ cup chopped onions

1 green pepper, chopped
3 cloves garlic, minced
6-ounce can tomato paste
1-pound can tomatoes
1 teaspoon sugar
1 teaspoon dried basil
Salt and pepper
1 cup grated Parmesan cheese

1. In chicken fryer put chicken and enough water to cover generously. Add quartered vegetables, parsley, bay leaf, and thyme. Bring to a boil, cover, and cook over low heat for 2 hours.
2. Strain and reserve liquid from chicken. Bone and skin chicken, and cut meat into small pieces.
3. Return strained liquid to chicken fryer and add water if necessary to make about 3 quarts liquid. Bring to a boil, add spaghetti, and cook for about 10 minutes, or until spaghetti is just barely tender.
4. Drain spaghetti, return to chicken fryer, and toss with half the olive oil. Set aside.
5. In 10-inch skillet heat remaining olive oil, and in it cook chopped onions, green pepper, and garlic for 10 min-

utes or until vegetables are tender, but not browned. Stir in tomato paste, tomatoes, sugar, and basil. Season with salt and pepper to taste. Bring to a boil and simmer for 30 minutes.

6. Preheat oven 350° F.

7. Sprinkle chicken over spaghetti in chicken fryer, and pour in tomato sauce. Sprinkle with cheese.

8. Bake in preheated oven for 45 minutes. Serve right in the chicken fryer.

JAMBALAYA
Serves 4

¼ cup butter
1 large clove garlic, minced
½ cup finely chopped onion
1 green pepper, seeded and chopped
1-pound 4-ounce can tomatoes

½ teaspoon salt
¼ teaspoon pepper
2 cups diced cooked ham
1 cup diced cooked shrimp
1½ cups chicken broth
1 cup raw rice

1. In chicken fryer melt butter, and in it sauté garlic and onion over moderate heat for about 3 minutes, stirring occasionally.

2. Add green pepper, tomatoes, salt, and pepper, and cook for 10 minutes longer, stirring occasionally.

3. Add ham, shrimp, broth, and rice. Bring liquid to a rapid boil. Cover fryer, reduce heat to low and cook for 25 minutes without lifting lid.

4.   Remove cover, fluff rice with a fork. If most of the liquid has not been absorbed, cover and cook for 5 minutes longer.

PINEAPPLE DUCKLING
Serves 4

5-pound duckling,
  quartered
1-pound 4½-ounce can
  cubed pineapple
1 tablespoon soy sauce
1 teaspoon gravy coloring
¼ teaspoon ginger
½ teaspoon salt

¼ teaspoon pepper
2 tablespoons butter
1 medium onion, finely
  chopped
1 medium green pepper,
  finely chopped
2 tablespoons cornstarch
¼ cup water

1.   Wipe duckling and cut off excess fat and skin. Arrange in shallow dish.

2.   Drain pineapple, reserving liquid. Mix liquid with soy sauce, gravy coloring, ginger, salt, and pepper. Pour mixture over duckling and marinate for at least 3 hours, turning duckling occasionally.

3.   Remove duckling from marinade and pat day. Reserve marinade.

4.   In chicken fryer melt butter, and in it sauté 2 pieces of duckling at a time until well browned on both sides. Set duckling aside.

5.   To fat remaining in pan add onion and green pepper, and sauté for 5 minutes. Stir in marinade and bring to a boil. Add duckling, cover, and cook over low heat for 1 hour.

6. Remove duckling to a warm serving platter and keep warm.

7. Blend cornstarch and water. Skim fat from liquid in pan, and stir cornstarch mixture into liquid. Cook, stirring constantly, until sauce is clear and thickened.

8. Add pineapple cubes, and simmer for 2 minutes.

9. Pour sauce and pineapple over duckling and serve.

OVEN-BARBECUED CHICKEN
Serves 6

½ cup flour
2 teaspoons salt
6 serving pieces frying
    chicken
¼ cup cooking oil
½ cup butter
1 cup chili sauce
½ cup water

¼ cup lemon juice
¼ cup minced onion
1 tablespoon
    Worcestershire sauce
2 tablespoons brown
    sugar
½ teaspoon paprika
½ teaspoon dry mustard

1. Mix flour and salt. Roll chicken pieces in the flour.

2. In chicken fryer heat oil and half the butter, and in it sauté chicken over medium heat until golden brown on all sides.

3. Preheat oven to 350° F.

4. In saucepan melt remaining butter and mix with chili sauce, water, lemon juice, onion, Worcestershire sauce, brown sugar, paprika, and mustard. Bring mixture to a boil and pour over chicken in fryer.

5. Cover fryer and bake chicken in the preheated oven for about 1 hour or until tender. Serve in the fryer.

LEG OF VEAL ITALIANO
Serves 6

2-pound piece of boned
leg of veal
Ham stuffing
2 tablespoons olive oil
1 quart beef stock or
bouillon
½ pound mushrooms,
chopped

½ cup chopped green
onions
Salt and pepper to
taste
1½ tablespoons
cornstarch
2 tablespoons water
Chopped parsley

1.   Make a pocket in the veal and fill it with ham stuffing. Sew pocket or secure with wooden picks.
2.   In chicken fryer heat oil and in it brown veal well on all sides.
3.   Add stock, mushrooms, green onions, and salt and pepper. Cover and simmer over low heat for 1½ hours, or until veal is tender.
4.   Remove veal from liquid, remove thread or picks, and slice veal thinly. Arrange slices on warm serving plate and keep warm.
5.   Strain liquid, pressing through the sieve as much of the vegetables as possible, and return liquid to chicken fryer.
6.   In cup or small bowl blend cornstarch with water. Stir mixture into liquid, and cook over low heat, stirring constantly, until sauce is smooth and thickened.
7.   Pour sauce over veal and sprinkle with parsley.

SICILIAN BRAISED SHOULDER OF VEAL
Serves 6

3-pound boned and
rolled shoulder of
veal
2 slices bacon, diced
2 cloves garlic, cut into
slivers
Crushed red pepper
1 tablespoon olive oil
2 carrots, diced

2 stalks celery, chopped
¼ pound fresh
mushrooms, chopped
1 cup beef stock or
consommé
1 cup dry white wine
Salt and pepper
1 tablespoon cornstarch
2 tablespoons water

1. Cut slits in veal about 2 inches apart. Insert a piece of bacon, a sliver of garlic and a few flakes of red pepper in each slit.
2. In chicken fryer heat oil and in it sear veal over high heat until well browned on all sides. Remove veal from pan. Add carrots, celery, and mushrooms to drippings in pan, and sauté for 5 minutes over moderate heat. Stir in stock and wine, and season to taste with salt and pepper. Bring liquid to a boil.
3. Replace veal in fryer, cover, and cook over low heat for 2 hours, turning meat occasionally.
4. Remove veal from fryer, slice thinly, and arrange slices on warm serving platter. Keep warm.
5. Strain liquid, pressing through sieve as much of the vegetables as possible, or blend in electric blender. Return liquid to fryer.
6. Blend cornstarch and water and stir into liquid. Cook, stirring constantly, until sauce is smooth and thickened. Pour sauce over veal and serve.

OSSO BUCO
Serves 4 to 6

2 meaty forelegs of veal,
    each cut into 3 pieces
⅓ cup flour
¼ cup olive oil
1 large onion, sliced
½ cup chopped celery
2 carrots, diced
½ cup dry white wine
1-pound, 13-ounce can
    tomatoes

1 tablespoon tomato
    paste
2 tablespoons chopped
    parsley
1 clove garlic, minced
Grated rind of 1 lemon
1 teaspoon salt
¼ teaspoon pepper
1 bay leaf

1. Preheat oven to 300° F.
2. Coat pieces of veal with flour, reserving any remaining flour.
3. In chicken fryer heat olive oil, and in it brown veal on all sides. Add onion, celery, and carrots, cover, and braise over low heat for 5 minutes.
4. Add wine and bring to a boil. Cook rapidly until wine has almost evaporated.
5. Sprinkle meat and vegetables with reserved flour, and stir in undrained tomatoes, tomato paste, parsley, garlic, lemon rind, salt, pepper, and bay leaf.
6. Bring liquid to a boil, cover chicken fryer, and bake in preheated oven for about 2½ hours, or until meat on bones is very tender.

NEVER-CURDLE BEEF STROGANOFF
Serves 6

¼ cup butter
2 pounds beef sirloin,
cut into thin,
finger-length slivers
2 cups thinly sliced
onions
½ pound mushrooms,
sliced

2 tablespoons flour
2 teaspoons sugar
2 teaspoons salt
¼ teaspoon pepper
8-ounce can tomato
sauce
1 cup commercial sour
cream

1. In 10-inch skillet melt butter. Add beef and onions, and sauté over moderate heat, until meat and onions are lightly browned.
2. Turn meat and onions into chicken fryer.
3. To juices remaining in skillet add mushrooms, and sauté for 5 minutes, or until mushrooms are limp. Sprinkle with flour, sugar, salt, and pepper. Stir in tomato sauce and bring to a boil, stirring constantly.
4. Pour tomato mixture over meat in chicken fryer. Cover and cook over low heat for 15 minutes.
5. Meanwhile stir sour cream into skillet and heat slowly, stirring constantly, until cream is warm.
6. Just before serving, stir sour cream into meat mixture. Serve with cooked rice.

POT ROAST WITH TOMATOES
Serves 6 to 8

2 tablespoons shortening
3 pounds boneless top
or bottom round of
beef
2 large onions, sliced
3 tablespoons flour
2½ teaspoons salt
¼ teaspoon pepper
1 teaspoon monosodium
glutamate

½ teaspoon dried basil
2 large ripe tomatoes,
peeled, seeded, and
diced
4 medium carrots, cut
into 2-inch lengths
12 small potatoes, peeled

1. In chicken fryer melt shortening, and in it brown meat well on all sides. Remove meat from pan and set aside.
2. Add onions to shortening remaining in fryer and cook until limp. Sprinkle onions with flour, salt, pepper, monosodium glutamate, and basil. Stir in tomatoes and bring to a boil.
3. Return meat to fryer. Cover and cook over low heat for 30 minutes. Add carrots and potatoes, and simmer for 2 hours longer, or until meat is tender.

TORTILLA PIE
Serves 6 to 8

1½ pounds ground beef
1 large onion, chopped
1 medium green pepper,
chopped
⅓ cup flour
1½ teaspoons salt
2 teaspoons chili powder
4 8-ounce cans tomato
sauce

2 cups water
½ cup finely chopped
stuffed olives
1 package (12) tortillas
4 cups grated Cheddar
cheese
6 hard-cooked eggs,
sliced

1. Preheat oven to 325° F. Grease a 4-quart chicken fryer.
2. In 12-inch skillet cook meat until it loses all red color.
Add onion and green pepper, and sauté for 5 minutes.
3. Sprinkle vegetables and meat with flour, salt, and chili
powder. Stir in tomato sauce, water, and olives. Simmer
for 5 minutes.
4. In chicken fryer arrange alternate layers of tortillas,
cheese, eggs, and sauce, finishing with sauce.
5. Bake in preheated oven for 1 hour. Serve right in the
chicken fryer.

BEST SWISS STEAK EVER
Serves 4

2 pounds round steak
cut 1¼ inches thick
1 clove garlic, halved
3 tablespoons flour
2 teaspoons salt
¼ teaspoon pepper
2 tablespoons shortening
1 large onion, sliced

4 medium fresh or
canned tomatoes,
sliced, or diced
2 carrots, sliced
½ cup sliced celery
¼ cup chopped green
pepper

1. Preheat oven to 325° F.
2. Rub steak on both sides with cut side of garlic. Chop and reserve garlic.
3. Pound flour, salt, and pepper into the steak with meat pounder or edge of a heavy plate.
4. In chicken fryer melt shortening and in it brown steak quickly on both sides.
5. Top steak with onion slices, tomatoes, carrots, celery, green pepper, and chopped garlic.
6. Cover and bake in preheated oven for 2 to 2½ hours.

RISOTTO WITH CHICKEN LIVERS
Serves 4

1 tablespoon olive oil
2 hot Italian sausages,
   thinly sliced
1 large onion, chopped
½ cup chopped celery
⅓ cup chopped green
   pepper
2 cups diced eggplant
2 cups sliced mushrooms

1 cup raw rice
2½ cups chicken broth
⅛ teaspoon saffron
1½ teaspoons salt
¼ teaspoon pepper
½ pound chicken livers,
   diced
Grated Parmesan cheese

1. Heat oil in chicken fryer, and in it sauté sausages until lightly browned.
2. Add onion, celery, and green pepper, and sauté over moderate heat for 5 minutes.
3. Stir in eggplant, mushrooms, and rice, and cook, stirring, until excess fat has been absorbed by rice.
4. Stir in broth, saffron, salt, and pepper, and bring to a boil.
5. Stir in chicken livers, cover, and cook over low heat for 20 minutes, or until all liquid is absorbed.
6. Serve in the chicken fryer with grated cheese.

SHRIMP CREOLE
Serves 8

¼ cup butter
1 medium onion,
  chopped
1 clove garlic, crushed
1 medium green pepper,
  chopped
1 cup chopped celery
1-pound 13-ounce can
  tomatoes

1½ teaspoon salt
¼ teaspoon pepper
¼ teaspoon dried basil
¼ teaspoon sugar
2 pounds raw shrimp,
  shelled and deveined
¼ cup chopped parsley

1. In chicken fryer melt butter, and in it sauté onion, garlic, green pepper, and celery for 5 minutes.
2. Add undrained tomatoes, salt, pepper, basil, and sugar, and bring to a boil. Simmer for 10 minutes.
3. Stir in shrimp, cover, and simmer for 10 minutes longer. Sprinkle with parsley.
4. Serve over bed of cooked rice.

SHRIMP PORTUGAISE
Serves 6

3 slices bacon, diced
1 medium onion, chopped
½ cup chopped green pepper
½ cup chopped celery
1 small bay leaf
2 tablespoons chopped parsley
¼ teaspoon sugar

½ teaspoon dried basil
1½ teaspoons salt
¼ teaspoon pepper
6 large tomatoes, peeled, seeded, and diced
2 pounds raw shrimp, shelled and deveined
1 cup fresh bread crumbs

1. In chicken fryer sauté bacon for 5 minutes. Add onion, green pepper, and celery and sauté until vegetables are limp, stirring frequently.
2. Add bay leaf, parsley, sugar, basil, salt, and pepper, and cook for 5 minutes longer.
3. Stir in tomatoes and shrimp, cover, and cook over low heat for 10 minutes.
4. Discard bay leaf. Sprinkle with crumbs and simmer for 2 minutes
5. Serve with cooked rice.

SEAFOOD PAELLA

Serves 4

¼ cup olive oil
½ cup chopped onions
⅓ cup chopped celery
¼ cup chopped green
  pepper
¼ cup chopped sweet
  red pepper or pimiento
1¼ cups raw rice
½ pound fresh
  mushrooms, sliced
½ small eggplant,
  chopped

3 cups water
1¼ teaspoons salt
¼ teaspoon saffron
1 pound raw shrimp,
  shelled and deveined
2 frozen rock lobster
  tails, poached, shelled,
  and diced
1 dozen mussels or
  cherrystone clams,
  scrubbed
Grated Parmesan cheese

1. In chicken fryer heat oil, and in it sauté onions, celery, green and red pepper for 10 minutes.
2. Stir in rice, and sauté for 5 minutes, stirring frequently.
3. Add mushrooms, eggplant, water, salt, and saffron. Cover and cook over low heat for 20 minutes, or until most of the liquid has been absorbed.
4. Stir in shrimp, cover, and cook for 5 minutes.
5. Stir in lobster, and arrange mussels or clams on top of rice mixture.
6. Cover and simmer for 8 minutes, or until shells have opened.
7. Serve in the chicken fryer with grated cheese on the side.

PEACHES IN WHITE WINE
Serves 6

3 *pounds or 12 fresh*
firm peaches
1 *cup sugar*

1 *cup dry white wine*
¼ *teaspoon cinnamon*

1. Peel peaches and leave whole.
2. In chicken fryer combine sugar, wine, and cinnamon, and bring to a boil.
3. Place peaches in syrup, cover, and cook over low heat for 15 minutes, or until peaches are just tender but still firm.
4. Remove peaches from syrup to a serving dish.
5. Boil syrup, uncovered, for 10 minutes, or until reduced to half the quantity.
6. Pour syrup over peaches and chill for at least 4 hours before serving.

SOUTHERN-FRIED CHICKEN WITH MILK GRAVY
Serves 4

2 *pounds shortening*
1½ *cups all-purpose flour*
2 *teaspoons salt*
⅛ *teaspoon black*
pepper

1 *teaspoon paprika*
2 *frying chickens, cut*
into serving portions
1 *cup hot water*
1 *cup milk*

1. In chicken fryer heat shortening to just below smoking point (365° F.).
2. In paper bag combine flour, salt, pepper, and paprika.

Add a few pieces of chicken at a time and shake well to coat the pieces. Reserve remaining flour mixture.

3. Place largest pieces of chicken in center of fryer and surround by smaller pieces. When all pieces are in the fryer, reduce heat a little. When chicken begins to brown on underside, cover fryer and cook for about 4 minutes. When golden brown underneath, turn and cook until golden brown all over. Total cooking time is about 30 minutes.

4. Remove chicken from fryer to absorbent paper to drain.

5. Make gravy: Pour off all but 3 tablespoons fat from fryer. Remove fryer from heat and stir in 4 tablespoons of reserved flour mixture. Cook over low heat, stirring constantly until mixture turns slightly brown. Add water and milk, and bring to a rapid boil, stirring constantly. Correct seasoning and serve gravy with the chicken.

BREADED FRIED FOODS

Fish fillets, oysters, scallops, soft-shelled crabs and so on are particularly good coated with fine bread crumbs or corn meal and deep fried. Serve with lemon wedges and tartar sauce.

TO BREAD

Beat 1 egg with 2 tablespoons water and pour into shallow dish like an open baker or pie plate. Sprinkle a square of waxed paper with flour; another heavily with bread crumbs or corn meal. Coat food first in flour, dip into beaten egg mixture, then roll in bread crumbs or corn meal. Fry in chicken fryer in 1 inch shortening or oil heated to 365° F. for about 5 minutes, or until golden brown. Drain on absorbent paper and sprinkle lightly with salt.

CRUMB-FRIED CHICKEN
Serves 2

½ cup milk
1 egg yolk
½ cup all-purpose flour
1½ teaspoons salt
1 teaspoon paprika
2½ pound frying
  chicken, cut into
  serving pieces

1 cup fresh bread crumbs
Shortening or oil for
  deep frying

1. Combine milk and egg yolk, stir in flour, salt, and paprika to make a smooth batter.
2. Dip each piece of chicken in egg mixture, then roll in crumbs. Place on cake rack to dry for a few minutes.
3. In chicken fryer put enough shortening or oil to measure about 1½ inches deep and heat to 365° F. Fry chicken pieces in the hot fat, a few at a time, for about 15 minutes, or until golden brown and tender. Drain on absorbent paper and keep warm in low oven until ready to serve.

MIXED FRY

Cauliflower flowerets, broccoli stalks, onions, artichoke hearts, eggplant, chicken livers, raw fish fillets, shrimp, Swiss cheese, and other small portions of foods.

1¼ cups sifted
   all-purpose flour
1 teaspoon salt
2 eggs, lightly beaten

1 cup milk
3 tablespoons melted
   butter or margarine

1. Prepare foods for frying: Hard vegetables such as cauliflower and broccoli should be parboiled for 5 minutes in boiling salted water and drained well. Defrost artichoke hearts or drain canned. Slice eggplant and cut into thin julienne strips. Clean livers and separate the halves. Slice onions ¼-inch thick and separate into rings, cut fish fillets into small portions, shell, devein, and butterfly shrimp, cut cheese into wedges or strips.
2. In mixing bowl combine flour and salt. Stir in eggs and milk. Stir in melted butter.
3. In chicken fryer, heat shortening or oil to a depth of 1 inch to 365° F.
4. Dip portions of food, a few at a time, into batter, and fry in the hot fat for 3 to 4 minutes, or until golden brown. Drain on absorbent paper. Sprinkle lightly with salt.
5. Keep warm in low oven until ready to serve. Serve with wedges of lemon.

DEEP-FRIED CRAB BALLS
Serves 3

2 *tablespoons butter or*
   margarine
2 *tablespoons flour*
⅓ *cup milk*
2 *egg yolks*
½ *teaspoon salt*
Dash mace
Dash cayenne
2 *tablespoons chopped*
   parsley

6-ounce package frozen
   Alaska king crab meat,
   thawed and flaked
Flour
1 *egg beaten with 2*
   tablespoons milk
¾ *cup fine dry bread*
   crumbs
Shortening for deep
   frying

1. In 2-quart saucepan melt butter or margarine and stir in the 2 tablespoons flour.
2. Gradually add milk, and cook over low heat, stirring constantly, until mixture is smooth and thick. Remove from heat and beat in egg yolks, salt, mace, and cayenne. Stir in parsley and crab meat and chill well.
3. Shape crab-meat mixture into balls about 1½ inches in diameter, and roll in flour. Dip into egg beaten with milk and roll in crumbs. Reshape if necessary.
4. In chicken fryer heat shortening or oil to a depth of 1 inch to 365° F. Fry crab-meat balls in the hot fat for 4 to 5 minutes, or until golden.
5. Drain on absorbent paper and serve with tartar sauce.

DEEP-FRIED POTATO BALLS
Serves 8

4 cups mashed potatoes
1 medium onion, grated
2 tablespoons soft butter
Salt and pepper
⅓ cup flour
2 eggs beaten with 2
    tablespoons milk

2¼ cups dry bread
    crumbs
Shortening for deep
    frying

1. Mix potatoes with onion and butter and season to taste with salt and pepper. Shape into 1-inch balls and roll in flour.
2. Dip potato balls into egg mixture, and coat in crumbs. Reshape if necessary.
3. In chicken fryer heat shortening or oil to a depth of 1 inch to 365° F. In it fry half the potato balls for 4 to 5 minutes, or until golden. Drain on absorbent paper and keep warm in low oven while frying remaining potato balls. Serve hot.

5

HALF A DOZEN DISHES
FOR EACH CASSEROLE

There's nothing new about casserole cooking. It is an ancient method, and the first primitive casseroles were fashioned of clay. Today they are made in a wide variety of metals, shapes, and sizes. The one requirement of a casserole is that it has a tight-fitting cover, for a dish to be called a casserole should, in the proper sense of the word, utilize this cover either part of the time or throughout the entire cooking process. Casserole cooking, whether done on top of the stove or in the oven, is a process of slow cooking in moist heat by which the food cooks with a minimum of attention, yet retains the maximum of flavor. All the juices and aromas are sealed within.

Many dishes are called casseroles, when they really are baking dishes, and for these we have used the shallow open baking dishes in a previous chapter. The one thing both these types of utensils have in common is that the food is usually served in the dish in which it was baked or braised.

Eventually you will want several deep casseroles, round or oval, with tight-fitting covers, in different colors and with different capacities. These would be:

1½-quart casserole for braising small quantities of vegetables and for some desserts.

2½- to 3-quart casserole for scalloped meats, fish, poultry, eggs and vegetables, for small quantities of boneless stews and ragouts.

4½- to 5½-quart casserole or Dutch oven for braising meats and poultry, for stews with the bones, such as oxtails and veal shanks, and for cooking bulky vegetables such as cabbage, artichokes, and whole potatoes.

7- to 8-quart casserole or Stock Pot for making soup bases, braising large roasts, whole poultry, for large quantities of stews and fish chowders, for cooking spaghetti or noodles. It can be used as a steamer for vegetables and puddings and makes a fine preserving kettle.

It's not likely that you will buy all these pieces of cookware at one time, since you are going to invest in heavy-durable, flameproof and ovenproof casseroles that withstand the test of time, conduct heat evenly, hold a constant internal temperature, and add to the décor of your kitchen and table.

The best size to begin with is an ample one with a capacity of 4½ to 5½ quarts, in which you can braise pot roasts, poach chickens, cook spaghetti or noodles and vegetables. It will be your Dutch oven and your cocotte in addition to a roomy casserole. Our next choice would be the still larger 7- to 8-quart casserole, which will be your "party" casserole, yet will double as a stock pot and a steamer. After that you can add as many casseroles as you wish.

1½-Quart Casseroles

CHEESE EGGS
Serves 4

¼ cup butter
2 tablespoons grated
  onion
¼ cup flour
¼ teaspoon dry mustard
1 teaspoon salt
¼ teaspoon pepper
2 cups milk

Dash Tabasco
2 cups grated Cheddar
  cheese
8 hard-cooked eggs,
  sliced
½ cup buttered bread
  crumbs

1. Preheat oven to 375° F. Grease 1½-quart casserole.
2. In 1½-quart saucepan melt butter, and in it sauté onion for 5 minutes. Stir in flour, mustard, salt, and pepper. Gradually stir in milk, and cook over medium heat, stirring constantly, until sauce is smooth and thickened.
3. Add Tabasco and cheese, and cook, stirring, until cheese is melted.
4. Arrange egg slices in casserole and pour cheese sauce over them. Sprinkle with buttered crumbs.
5. Bake in preheated oven for 30 minutes. Serve in the casserole.

RATATOUILLE NICOISE
Serves 6

1 *medium eggplant,*
　thinly sliced
Salt
Olive oil
1 *large onion, chopped*
1 *clove garlic, minced*
1 *cup chopped celery*
½ *cup chopped green*
　pepper

¼ *pound fresh*
　mushrooms, sliced
3 *pounds tomatoes,*
　peeled, seeded, and
　diced
Salt and pepper to taste
½ *cup chopped parsley*

1.　Put eggplant slices in a bowl, sprinkling each layer lightly with salt. Let stand 30 minutes, then drain and wipe each slice dry with absorbent paper.

2.　In 10-inch skillet heat about 2 tablespoons oil and in it sauté a few eggplant slices on both sides until lightly brown. Set aside and continue sautéing eggplant slices until all are cooked, adding more oil to the skillet as needed.

3.　Add 3 tablespoons oil to skillet, and heat. In it sauté onion, garlic, celery, and green pepper over moderate heat for 5 minutes, stirring occasionally. Add mushrooms and tomatoes and season generously with salt and pepper. Bring to a boil and cook over high heat for 15 minutes, or until excess liquid has evaporated.

4.　Meanwhile preheat oven to 350° F. Grease 1½-quart casserole.

5.　Spread about ⅓ of the tomato mixture in bottom of casserole. Overlap half the eggplant slices on top of tomato mixture and sprinkle with ⅓ of the parsley. Add another ⅓ of tomato mixture, and top with remaining eggplant.

Sprinkle with another ⅓ of the parsley. Cover eggplant slices with remaining tomato mixture and sprinkle with remaining parsley.

6. Cover and bake in preheated oven for 30 minutes. Serve in the casserole, hot as a vegetable or cold as an appetizer.

HAM AND SPINACH CASSEROLE
Serves 6

2 10-ounce packages frozen chopped spinach	½ cup ground ham
	Dash nutmeg
	¼ cup heavy cream
2 tablespoons butter	Salt and pepper
1 medium onion, grated or minced	¼ cup dry bread crumbs

1. Preheat oven to 375° F. Grease 1½-quart casserole.
2. Cook spinach according to package directions. Drain well and set aside.
3. In 10-inch skillet melt butter and in it sauté onion for 5 minutes. Remove from heat and stir in ham, nutmeg, and cream.
4. Mix ham mixture with spinach, and season with salt and pepper to taste.
5. Turn mixture into casserole and sprinkle with crumbs.
6. Bake in preheated oven for 20 minutes, or until crumbs are golden.

VEGETABLE BAKE
Serves 6 to 8

1 small eggplant, peeled
  and sliced
3 tablespoons olive oil
6 tablespoons butter
1 large onion, thinly
  sliced
1 cup chopped celery
1 medium green pepper,
  seeded and chopped

½ pound fresh
  mushrooms, sliced
¼ cup chopped parsley
3 tablespoons tomato
  paste
¼ teaspoon dried basil
Dash sugar
Salt and pepper
¼ cup fresh bread
  crumbs

1.   Preheat oven to 375° F. Grease 1½-quart casserole.
2.   In 10-inch skillet heat oil, and in it sauté eggplant slices until golden brown on both sides. Drain slices as they finish cooking on absorbent paper.
3.   Arrange half the eggplant slices in bottom of casserole.
4.   In skillet melt 3 tablespoons butter, and in it sauté onion, celery, and green pepper over moderate heat for 5 minutes. Add mushrooms, and sauté for 5 minutes longer, stirring frequently.
5.   Stir in parsley, tomato paste, basil, and sugar, and season to taste with salt and pepper.
6.   Turn vegetable mixture into casserole and top with remaining eggplant slices.
7.   Cover and bake in preheated oven for 25 minutes. Remove from oven and turn oven to broil.
8.   In skillet melt remaining butter, and stir in crumbs. Remove cover from casserole. Sprinkle crumbs on top of vegetables and broil 4 to 5 inches from source of heat for 5 minutes, or until top is crusty and golden.

WALNUT RICE
Serves 4 to 6

¼ cup butter
1 medium onion,
   chopped
½ cup chopped green
   pepper
1 cup raw rice

2½ cups chicken broth
2 teaspoons salt
¼ teaspoon pepper
¼ teaspoon ginger
½ teaspoon paprika
½ cup chopped walnuts

1.   Preheat oven to 350° F.
2.   In 10-inch skillet melt butter, and in it sauté onion and green pepper over moderate heat for 5 minutes. Add rice, and sauté for 5 minutes longer, stirring frequently.
3.   Add broth, salt, pepper, ginger, paprika, and walnuts, and bring broth to a boil.
4.   Pour into 1½-quart casserole. Cover and bake 35 minutes in preheated oven, or until all liquid is absorbed.
5.   Serve in the casserole with fried chicken, with pineapple duckling (see index) or as you wish.

WILD RICE CASSEROLE
Serves 6

½ cup butter
1 medium onion, grated
   or minced
½ cup finely chopped
   celery
¼ cup fresh mushrooms,
   sliced

¼ cup slivered almonds
   or water chestnuts
3½ cups cooked wild
   rice
1 teaspoon salt
¼ teaspoon pepper

1.   Preheat oven to 350° F. Grease 1½-quart casserole.

2. In 12-inch skillet melt butter, and in it sauté onion and celery for 10 minutes. Add mushrooms, and sauté for 5 minutes, or until mushrooms are limp, stirring frequently.

3. Remove skillet from heat and stir in almonds, rice, salt, and pepper. Turn into casserole.

4. Cover casserole and bake in preheated oven for 25 minutes. Serve in the casserole.

APPLE CRUMBLE

Serves 4 to 6

1 cup all-purpose flour
Dash salt
¼ teaspoon ground cloves
½ teaspoon cinnamon
1 cup firmly packed brown sugar

½ cup butter
6 medium apples, peeled, cored, and sliced
1 tablespoon lemon juice

1. Preheat oven to 350° F. Grease 1½-quart casserole.

2. Sift flour, salt, cloves, and cinnamon into mixing bowl. Add ¾ cup sugar and cut in butter until mixture resembles coarse bread crumbs.

3. Sprinkle about ⅓ of the crumb mixture in bottom of casserole.

4. Mix apples and lemon juice and empty into casserole over crumbs. Top with remaining crumb mixture and sprinkle with remaining ¼ cup sugar.

5. Cover casserole and bake in preheated oven for 30

minutes. Remove cover and continue to bake for 20 minutes longer.

6. Serve warm in the casserole with whipped cream or ice cream.

SOUTHERN BREAD PUDDING
Serves 4

6 slices buttered bread,
    cut into 2-inch squares
½ cup seedless raisins
⅓ cup chopped pecans
2 eggs, separated
¾ cup firmly packed
    brown sugar

2 cups milk
1 teaspoon vanilla
Dash salt
2 tablespoons granulated
    sugar

1. Preheat oven to 350° F. Grease 1½-quart casserole.
2. Arrange half the bread squares in bottom of casserole and sprinkle with half the raisins and pecans.
3. Top with remaining bread squares, raisins, and pecans.
4. In mixing bowl blend egg yolks with brown sugar, milk, vanilla, and salt. Pour milk mixture over bread in casserole.
5. Cover and bake in preheated oven for 55 minutes.
6. Beat egg whites until foamy and gradually beat in granulated sugar. Continue to beat until meringue is stiff and glossy.
7. Remove cover from casserole and spread beaten egg whites on top. Bake for 15 minutes longer. Serve hot or warm with cream.

SURPRISE RICE PUDDING
Serves 6

1-pound can apricot halves	¾ cup sugar
	Dash salt
1½ cups milk	Grated rind of 1 lemon
3 eggs, separated	3 cups cooked rice

1. Preheat oven to 350° F. Grease 1½-quart casserole.
2. Drain apricots, reserving ½ cup syrup.
3. Combine milk, egg yolks, the reserved syrup, ½ cup of the sugar, salt, and lemon rind.
4. Put rice in prepared pan, and pour in the milk mixture. Cover and bake in preheated oven for 1 hour.
5. Beat egg whites until foamy. Gradually beat in remaining ¼ cup sugar, and continue to beat until meringue is stiff and glossy.
6. Remove cover from casserole. Arrange apricot halves on top of pudding. Cover completely with meringue. Return to oven and bake for 20 minutes longer.

2½- Quart Casserole

BARBECUED ROAST CHICKEN
Serves 4

1 tablespoon melted butter	¼ cup prepared barbecue sauce
1 teaspoon salt	3½-pound roasting chicken
¼ teaspoon pepper	

1. Preheat oven to 375° F. Grease 2½-quart casserole.
2. In small bowl or cup blend melted butter, salt, pepper, and barbecue sauce.
3. Put chicken in casserole, breast side up, and brush with half the prepared sauce. Cover and bake in preheated oven for 2 hours.
4. Remove cover, baste with remaining sauce, and roast for 30 minutes longer.

CHICKEN PROVENCALE
Serves 4

3½-pound broiler-fryer chicken, cut into serving pieces
Cornstarch
3 slices bacon, diced
1 medium onion, chopped
1 clove garlic, minced
3 pounds or 3 large tomatoes, peeled, seeded, and diced
1½ teaspoons salt
¼ teaspoon pepper
1 cup chicken stock
2 tablespoons chopped parsley

1. Preheat oven to 375° F.
2. Coat chicken pieces lightly in cornstarch and set aside.
3. In 10-inch skillet sauté bacon until crisp. Remove bacon from skillet, leaving fat in skillet. Set bacon aside.
4. Sauté chicken pieces in skillet until golden on both sides. Put chicken in 2½-quart casserole and sprinkle with bacon.
5. In fat remaining in skillet sauté onion and garlic over moderate heat for 5 minutes. Add tomatoes and simmer for 5 minutes. Stir in salt, pepper, and stock, and bring to a boil.

6.   Pour tomato mixture over chicken, cover casserole, and bake in preheated oven for 45 minutes to 1 hour, or until chicken is tender.

7.   Serve in the casserole. Just before serving sprinkle with parsley and serve with cooked rice.

CHICKEN BREASTS IN CHICKEN LIVER SAUCE
Serves 6

3 tablespoons butter	2 tablespoons flour
3 large chicken breasts, boned and halved	1 teaspoon paprika
	1½ teaspoons salt
3 small shallots or green onions, chopped	¼ teaspoon pepper
	¼ teaspoon dried
¼ pound chicken livers, diced	tarragon
	1 cup chicken stock
¼ pound mushrooms, chopped	

1.   Preheat oven to 325° F. Grease 2½-quart casserole.

2.   In 12-inch skillet melt butter, and in it sauté chicken breasts lightly on both sides. Arrange chicken breasts in prepared casserole.

3.   Add shallots or green onions and chicken livers to butter remaining in skillet, and sauté just until chicken livers change color. Add mushrooms, and cook over low heat, stirring, for 3 minutes. Sprinkle with flour, paprika, salt, pepper, and tarragon.

4.   Gradually stir in chicken stock, and cook, stirring constantly, until sauce comes to a boil.

5.   Pour sauce into casserole. Cover and bake in preheated oven for 30 minutes. Serve right in the casserole.

EASY IRISH STEW
Serves 6

2 *pounds lean boned*
  and cubed leg of lamb
4 *cups sliced potatoes*
2 *cups sliced onions*
1 *cup boiling water*

1 *tablespoon salt*
¼ *teaspoon pepper*
2 *tablespoons chopped*
  parsley

1. Preheat oven to 325° F. Grease 2½-quart casserole.
2. Arrange alternate layers of lamb, potatoes, and onions in casserole.
3. Mix water with salt and pepper and add to casserole. Cover and bake in preheated oven for 2½ hours.
4. Remove cover and stir gently. Sprinkle with parsley and serve.

FLAVORFUL BEEF
Serves 6

1 *medium onion, grated*
  or minced
3 *sprigs fresh mint,*
  chopped
2 *tablespoons chopped*
  parsley
1½ *teaspoons salt*
¼ *teaspoon pepper*
2 *tablespoons olive oil*

1 *teaspoon Worcestershire*
  sauce
¼ *teaspoon dried*
  tarragon
½ *cup dry red wine*
3½- *to 4-pound rolled*
  rib roast
2 *tablespoons shortening*

1. In 2½-quart casserole combine onion, mint, parsley, salt, pepper, oil, Worcestershire sauce, tarragon, and wine.

2. Place beef in the casserole, and let marinate for at least 6 hours, or overnight, turning beef occasionally.
3. Preheat oven to 350° F.
4. Remove beef from casserole and wipe dry. Pour marinade from casserole into bowl or cup and set aside. Wash and dry casserole.
5. Return beef to casserole and dot with shortening. Bake in preheated oven for 2 hours or until beef is done to taste, basting occasionally with the marinade during baking period.

BOSTON FISH PIE
Serves 4

½ cup water
Salt and pepper
1 small bay leaf
½ pound fillet of
flounder or haddock
½ pound shrimp, shelled
and deveined
½ pound bay scallops
Light cream
½ cup butter
⅓ cup chopped celery
¼ cup chopped green
pepper

¼ cup flour
½ cup cooked whole
kernel corn
2 tablespoons chopped
parsley
1 tablespoon dry
vermouth
2 pounds potatoes,
cooked and mashed
2 tablespoons milk

1. In 2-quart saucepan combine water, ½ teaspoon salt, dash pepper, and bay leaf. Bring to a boil. Add fish and shrimp. Cover and cook over low heat for 5 minutes.
2. Add scallops. Cover and cook over low heat for 5 minutes longer.

3. Drain fish and reserve liquid. Discard bay leaf, flake fillets, and set aside with shrimp and scallops.

4. Add sufficient cream to fish liquid to make 1½ cups total. Set aside.

5. Preheat oven to 375° F. Grease 2½-quart casserole.

6. Make sauce: In 2-quart saucepan melt ¼ cup butter. Add celery and green pepper, and sauté over low heat for 10 minutes. Sprinkle vegetables with flour and gradually stir in reserved liquid. Cook, stirring constantly, until sauce is smooth and thickened. Season to taste with salt and pepper. Remove from heat and stir in corn, parsley, vermouth, fish, shrimp, and scallops.

7. Turn into prepared casserole.

8. Whip potatoes with remaining ¼ cup butter and milk.

9. Spoon potatoes on top of fish mixture in casserole and mark with tines of fork.

10. Bake in preheated oven for 25 minutes, or until potatoes are lightly brown.

CHEESE AND ONION SOUFFLE

Serves 4

3 tablespoons butter
3 tablespoons flour
½ teaspoon dry mustard
Dash cayenne
1 teaspoon crushed onion
  flakes
¾ teaspoon salt
¼ teaspoon pepper

1 cup milk
⅓ cup grated
  Parmesan cheese
1½ cups shredded sharp
  Cheddar cheese
4 egg yolks
6 egg whites

1. Preheat oven to 350° F.

2. In 2-quart saucepan melt butter. Stir in flour, mustard,

cayenne, onion flakes, salt, and pepper. Gradually stir in milk, and cook over moderate heat, stirring constantly, until sauce is smooth and thickened.

3.   Add cheese, and cook, stirring, until cheese is melted.

4.   Remove saucepan from heat and beat in egg yolks, one at a time.

5.   Meanwhile beat egg whites until stiff, but not dry. Fold beaten egg whites into egg-yolk mixture and turn into a 2½-quart casserole.

6.   Bake in preheated oven for 40 minutes. Serve at once.

2½- or 3-Quart Casserole

BEEF AND NOODLE HASH
Serves 6

4 slices bacon	1 teaspoon salt
1½ pounds ground beef	1 tablespoon
½ cup finely chopped	Worcestershire sauce
green onions	2 cups grated Cheddar
½ cup finely chopped	cheese
green pepper	12-ounce package medium
⅓ cup finely chopped	egg noodles, cooked
celery	and drained
4-ounce can mushrooms	½ cup fresh bread
8-ounce can tomato	crumbs
sauce	

1.   Preheat oven to 350° F. Grease a 2½- or 3-quart casserole.

2. In 12-inch skillet cook bacon until crisp. Remove bacon to absorbent paper to drain.

3. In bacon fat remaining in skillet cook beef, green onions, green pepper, and celery until beef loses all red color.

4. Stir in undrained mushrooms, tomato sauce, salt, and Worcestershire sauce. Bring to a boil and simmer for 10 minutes.

5. Remove from heat and stir in 1 cup cheese and the noodles. Crumble and stir in the crisp bacon.

6. Turn mixture into prepared casserole, and sprinkle with remaining 1 cup cheese mixed with the bread crumbs.

7. Bake in preheated oven for 40 minutes.

PORK AND NOODLES
Serves 6

1 *pound lean ground pork*
½ *pound ground beef*
2 *large onions, chopped*
2 *medium green peppers, chopped*
1 *clove garlic, minced*
2 *tablespoons flour*
1½ *teaspoons salt*
¼ *teaspoon pepper*

2 *1-pound 4-ounce cans tomatoes*
1 *teaspoon Worcestershire sauce*
12-*ounce package medium egg noodles, cooked, drained, and rinsed*
1 *cup grated Cheddar cheese*

1. In 12-inch skillet brown pork and beef. Add onions, green peppers, and garlic, and sauté for 5 minutes.

2. Sprinkle meat with flour, salt, and pepper. Stir in un-

drained tomatoes and Worcestershire. Simmer for 30 minutes.

3.   Preheat oven to 350° F. Grease 3-quart casserole.

4.   Mix meat with noodles and turn into prepared casserole.

5.   Sprinkle with cheese and bake in preheated oven for 40 minutes.

3-Quart Casserole

BAKED SPAGHETTI WITH SAUCE
Serves 6 to 8

1 tablespoon cooking oil
1½ tablespoons ground beef
1 cup finely chopped onions
2 cups tomato juice
6-ounce can tomato paste
2 bay leaves, crumbled
1 teaspoon dried basil
1 teaspoon sugar

2 teaspoons salt
¼ teaspoon pepper
1 pound spaghetti, cooked, drained, and rinsed
4-ounce can chopped mushrooms
½ cup sliced stuffed olives
2 cups grated Cheddar cheese

1.   In large skillet heat oil, and in it cook beef and onions until beef loses all red color and onions are transparent.

2.   Stir in tomato juice, tomato paste, bay leaves, basil, sugar, salt, and pepper. Bring to a boil, cover, and cook over low heat for 20 minutes.

3. Preheat oven to 350° F. Oil a 3-quart casserole.
4. Stir spaghetti, undrained mushrooms, olives, and 1 cup cheese into meat sauce and turn into prepared casserole.
5. Sprinkle with remaining 1 cup cheese. Bake in preheated oven for 30 minutes.

4½- or 5-Quart Casserole

POT AU FEU
Serves 6 to 8

4 pounds boneless beef
   rump, tied
2 quarts good beef stock
Few sprigs parsley
1 bay leaf
Pinch of thyme
1 large onion, sliced
2 stalks celery, sliced
2 carrots, sliced

1 tablespoon salt
2 leeks, cut into 3-inch
   lengths
4 carrots, cut into 3-
   inch lengths
1 small turnip, peeled
   and cut into 2-inch
   cubes
8 small whole onions

1. Place beef in casserole and cover with stock. Add parsley, bay leaf, thyme, sliced onion, celery, sliced carrots, and salt. Bring liquid to a boil, then cover and cook over very low heat for 2½ hours.
2. Add the chunks of leeks, carrots, turnip, and the whole onions. Cover and continue to cook over very low heat for 1 hour.

REAL BAKED BEANS
Serves 6 to 8

1 *pound dried pea or*
   navy beans
2 *quarts water*
¾ *cup firmly packed*
   brown sugar
¼ *cup molasses*

1 *tablespoon salt*
1 *tablespoon dry mustard*
1 *large onion, chopped*
2 *tablespoons tomato*
   paste
¼ *pound salt pork*

1. Soak beans overnight in water to cover by several inches in casserole in which they will be cooked and baked.
2. Next day bring water and beans to a boil, cover, and simmer for 1 hour.
3. Preheat oven to 300° F.
4. Drain liquid from beans, and reserve 2 cups.
5. To beans in casserole add sugar, molasses, salt, mustard, onion, tomato paste, and 2 cups of the reserved liquid.
6. Bury pork in center of bean mixture and cover casserole tightly.
7. Bake in preheated oven for 4 hours, stirring occasionally and adding more bean liquid or water if beans become too dry. Remove cover for last 30 minutes of cooking to brown beans.

5-Quart Casserole

BEEF IN RED WINE
Serves 6

¼ cup olive oil

4 pounds lean beef chuck, cut into 2-inch cubes

¼ cup brandy

1 large onion, finely chopped

½ cup finely chopped celery

¼ cup flour

2 teaspoons salt

¼ teaspoon pepper

1 bottle burgundy wine

1 bay leaf

2 tablespoons tomato paste

3 tablespoons butter

18 small onions, peeled

6 carrots, scraped and halved lengthwise

½ pound fresh mushroom caps

1. In 12-inch skillet heat half the olive oil and in it sear half the meat quickly on all sides over high heat. Transfer meat to a 5-quart casserole and repeat with rest of oil and meat.

2. Sprinkle with brandy and set alight. Let flame burn out.

3. Preheat oven to 325° F.

4. To oil and juices remaining in skillet add onion and celery, and sauté for 5 minutes, stirring occasionally. Sprinkle vegetables with flour, salt, and pepper. Gradually stir in wine, and cook, stirring constantly, until mixture comes to a boil. Add bay leaf, stir in tomato paste, and pour mixture over meat.

5. Cover casserole and bake in preheated oven for 2 hours.
6. Meanwhile melt butter in 10-inch skillet and in it brown onions on all sides. Add onions and carrots to casserole, cover, and bake for 40 minutes longer.
7. Add mushrooms, cover, and bake for 20 minutes longer. Serve in the casserole.

CHILI CON CARNE
Serves 12

3 pounds ground lean
  beef
3 large onions, chopped
1 green pepper, chopped
2 2-pound 3-ounce cans
  tomatoes with juice
¼ cup chili powder
1 bay leaf

1 teaspoon celery seed
2 teaspoons hot chili
  peppers, crushed
1 teaspoon dried basil
1 tablespoon salt
2 1-pound 4-ounce
  cans red kidney beans,
  drained

1. In a 5-quart flameproof casserole brown beef with onions over direct heat, stirring frequently, until onions are transparent and meat has lost all red color.
2. Add green pepper, tomatoes, chili powder, bay leaf, celery seed, chili peppers, basil, and salt. Bring to a boil and simmer, uncovered, over low heat for 2 hours, stirring occasionally.
3. Add beans, and simmer for 5 minutes longer before serving in the casserole.

CHICKEN EN COCOTTE
Serves 4

6 slices bacon, diced
4-pound roasting chicken,
  ready to cook and
  trussed
12 small new potatoes,
  peeled
4 medium carrots,
  scraped and quartered

12 small white onions,
  peeled
1 bay leaf
Few sprigs parsley
¼ teaspoon thyme
1½ teaspoons salt
⅓ cup dry white wine

1. In 5-quart flameproof casserole over direct heat cook bacon until crisp. Remove bacon from casserole and set aside.
2. Brown chicken carefully in bacon fat remaining in casserole, until golden on all sides. While chicken is browning, cook potatoes and carrots in 2-quart saucepan in boiling salted water for 5 minutes. Drain well.
3. Preheat oven to 325° F.
4. Remove chicken from casserole and brown potatoes lightly on all sides in fat in casserole. Push potatoes to sides of casserole and place chicken in center. Surround with carrots and onions. Add bay leaf, parsley, and thyme, and sprinkle chicken with salt.
5. Sprinkle bacon over vegetables, and pour wine over chicken. Bring liquid to a boil, cover casserole, and bake in preheated oven for 1 hour and 40 minutes, or until chicken is tender. Baste chicken occasionally during the cooking period. Serve in the casserole.

MOIST-ROASTED CHICKEN
Serves 6

5-pound roasting chicken, ready to cook	1 lemon, halved
	1 medium onion, halved
Salt and pepper	5 slices bacon

1. Preheat oven to 325° F. Grease 5-quart casserole.
2. Sprinkle inside of chicken with salt and pepper, and put lemon and onion halves in cavity. Truss chicken and place in casserole, breast side up.
3. Sprinkle outside of chicken with salt and pepper, and arrange bacon slices over the breast. Cover and bake in preheated oven for 2 hours.
4. Uncover and remove bacon slices. Bake for 30 minutes longer, uncovered, basting occasionally with liquids in bottom of pan.
5. Untruss and serve hot or cool, thinly sliced. It's delicious either way.

GLAZED SALMON
Serves 8

1 large onion, sliced	½ teaspoon salt
1 stalk celery, diced	4 pound center-cut fresh salmon
1 large carrot, sliced	
4 cups water	1 envelope plain gelatin
2 cups dry white wine	½ cup mayonnaise
1 bay leaf	Garnishes: pimiento, ripe olives, cucumber, parsley
Few sprigs parsley	
¼ teaspoon peppercorns	

1.   In 5-quart flameproof casserole put onion, celery, carrot, water, wine, bay leaf, parsley sprigs, peppercorns, and salt. Bring to a boil, cover and simmer for 30 minutes.

2.   Meanwhile wash salmon and remove any remaining scales. Wrap it tightly in a square of cheesecloth or a kitchen towel.

3.   Lower salmon gently into hot liquid in casserole. Cover and cook over very low heat for 1 hour.

4.   Remove casserole from heat and cool for 30 minutes. Remove salmon from liquid, unwrap, and chill.

5.   Boil liquid remaining in casserole over high heat until reduced to 2 cups. Strain and cool.

6.   In small saucepan combine gelatin with ½ cup of the cooled liquid. Stir over low heat until gelatin is thoroughly dissolved and mixture is clear. Stir this dissolved gelatin into remaining liquid. Stir in mayonnaise and beat until smooth. Let cool until mixture starts to thicken.

7.   Meanwhile carefully open salmon and remove bones. Replace salmon halves and discard skin. Place salmon on a wire rack with a plate or baking sheet underneath.

8.   Spoon some of the mayonnaise mixture over the salmon to coat it lightly. Chill until firm. Stir remaining mayonnaise mixture frequently to prevent it from setting. Give the salmon about 3 coats of the mayonnaise, spooning excess mayonnaise from the plate beneath and stirring it into rest of mayonnaise.

9.   Arrange salmon on cold serving plate, and garnish with pimiento strips, olive and cucumber slices, and sprays of parsley. Chill until ready to serve.

HEARTY POTATO SOUP
Serves 6

2 quarts good chicken
   or turkey stock
6 large potatoes, diced
1 medium carrot, diced
1 stalk celery, diced

3 medium onions, sliced
2 teaspoons salt
White pepper
1 quart milk

1. In 5-quart flameproof casserole put stock, potatoes, carrot, celery, onions, and salt. Bring to a boil, cover, and simmer over low heat for 1 hour.
2. Add milk, season to taste with salt and pepper, and heat to serving temperature.

GERMAN POTATO SALAD
Serves 8 to 10

4 pounds potatoes,
   peeled
½ pound sliced bacon,
   diced
1 large onion, chopped
3 tablespoons flour
½ cup cider vinegar

½ cup water
1 tablespoon prepared
   mustard
1 teaspoon celery seed
Salt and pepper
¼ cup chopped parsley

1. In 3-quart saucepan cook potatoes in boiling salted water until tender. Drain and keep warm.
2. Meanwhile in 5-quart flameproof casserole sauté bacon over moderate heat for 5 minutes or until golden. Add onion, and sauté for 10 minutes longer, stirring occasionally.

3. Sprinkle onion and bacon with flour, and stir in vinegar, water, and mustard. Cook, stirring constantly, until thickened.

4. Add celery seed. Slice potatoes into the casserole and mix lightly. Season generously with salt and pepper. Sprinkle with parsley and serve warm.

PARTY MEAT BALLS

Makes about 50 meat balls

2 cups fresh bread crumbs	1 teaspoon salt
1½ cups milk	¼ teaspoon pepper
1 large onion, grated	¼ teaspoon mace
1½ pounds ground beef	¾ cup flour
½ pound ground veal	¼ cup olive oil
½ pound ground pork	¼ cup butter
¼ cup chopped parsley	1 cup beef bouillon
2 eggs, beaten	2 cups light cream

1. In mixing bowl soak crumbs in milk for 10 minutes. Add onion, beef, veal, pork, parsley, eggs, salt, pepper, and mace. Mix well and shape into 1-inch balls.

2. Coat balls in flour and reserve remaining flour for sauce.

3. In 10-inch skillet heat about 1 tablespoon each oil and butter. Put about 30 meat balls in the skillet, and sauté over medium heat for 10 minutes, shaking skillet frequently to turn balls and brown them lightly on all sides. Place cooked balls in a 5-quart casserole, and continue to cook meat balls until all are done, adding oil and butter in equal proportions as needed.

4. Preheat oven to 350° F.

5. When all meat balls are browned, sprinkle reserved flour into fat and juices in skillet, and cook, stirring, until flour is lightly browned.

6. Gradually stir in bouillon, and cook over moderate heat, stirring in all brown bits from bottom and sides of skillet, until sauce is thickened.

7. Gradually stir in cream, and heat to simmering point.

8. Pour sauce over meat balls in casserole, cover, and bake in preheated oven for 30 minutes. Serve right in the casserole.

7- or 8-Quart Casserole or Stock Pot

GOOD TURKEY OR CHICKEN STOCK
Makes about 2 quarts

1 turkey or chicken carcass, with skin and some meat
1 stalk celery with leaves, quartered
2 carrots, quartered
3 medium onions, quartered

Few sprigs parsley
1 bay leaf
¼ teaspoon thyme
¼ teaspoon peppercorns
1 tablespoon salt

1. Break carcass into pieces and put into largest casserole. Add celery, carrots, onions, and sufficient water to come to within 2 inches of top of casserole.

2. Bring liquid to a boil, skimming off foam that rises to surface occasionally. Add parsley, bay leaf, thyme, peppercorns, and salt. Cover and cook over low heat for 6 to 8 hours.

3. Strain and use as desired. This stock freezes well.

STUFFING FOR ROAST OR POACHED CHICKEN
Serves 6 to 8

1 *large onion, shredded*
  or finely chopped
2 *cups chopped beef*
  suet from your butcher

4 *cups instant oatmeal*
2 *teaspoons salt*
¼ *teaspoon pepper*
¼ *cup water*

1. Grease a 1½-quart ovenproof bowl.
2. In large mixing bowl combine onion, suet, oatmeal, salt, pepper, and water. Pack into greased bowl and cover with waxed paper and then foil.
3. Place bowl in a 7- to 8-quart casserole or stock pot, and add sufficient water to come halfway up sides of bowl.
4. Cover tightly and simmer over moderate heat for 2 hours, adding more boiling water as necessary.
5. Unmold and serve hot.

STEAMED CHOCOLATE PUDDING CAKE
Serves 6 to 8

2 *cups all-purpose flour*
2 *teaspoons baking*
  powder
¼ *teaspoon salt*
½ *cup cocoa powder*
½ *cup butter*
½ *cup granulated sugar*

4 *eggs*
1 *cup milk*
1½ *cups fresh bread*
  crumbs
Chocolate sauce (see
  Index)

1. Grease 1½-quart ovenproof bowl or casserole.

2.   Sift flour, baking powder, salt, and cocoa onto piece of wax paper.

3.   In large mixing bowl cream butter and sugar until mixture is light and fluffy. Add eggs, one at a time, alternately with half the flour mixture, beating well after each addition.

4.   Add milk alternately with remaining flour and beat until smooth.

5.   Stir in crumbs and turn mixture into greased bowl. Cover bowl with foil and secure with string.

6.   Place bowl in a 7- or 8-quart casserole or stock pot and add sufficient boiling water to come halfway up sides of bowl.

7.   Cover and steam over moderate heat for 2½ hours, adding more water to the pan as needed.

9.   Unmold pudding cake onto serving dish and serve hot with chocolate sauce.

APPLE CHUTNEY
Makes about 3 quarts

1 quart red wine vinegar
4 cups firmly packed
   brown sugar
2 cloves garlic, minced
2 cups chopped onions
2 cups chopped celery
10 cups chopped peeled
   cored apples
1 tablespoon salt
2 tablespoons whole
   white mustard seeds

2 tablespoons chili
   powder
½ teaspoon crushed hot
   red pepper pods
½ teaspoon powdered
   cloves
1 teaspoon allspice
1 pound seedless raisins

1. Put all ingredients into a 7- or 8-quart stock pot or casserole. Bring to a boil and simmer over low heat for 1 hour stirring occasionally.
2. Turn into hot clean jars and seal at once.

CHRISTMAS PLUM PUDDING
Serves 8

¼ cup all-purpose flour
2 cups fresh bread crumbs
½ cup granulated sugar
1 cup finely chopped beef suet
1 cup seedless raisins
¾ cup currants
1 cup seedless white raisins
½ cup chopped almonds
½ cup mixed candied fruit peel
¼ cup chopped glacé cherries

¼ cup chopped candied lemon peel
⅛ teaspoon each cinnamon, ginger, mace, and nutmeg
¼ teaspoon salt
2 eggs
¼ cup milk
½ cup brandy
1 tablespoon lemon juice
1 teaspoon grated lemon rind
1 medium apple, cored and chopped

1. Grease 1½-quart ovenproof bowl or casserole.
2. In large mixing bowl combine flour, crumbs, sugar, suet, raisins, currants, white raisins, almonds, candied peel, cherries, candied lemon peel, spices, and salt. Mix well.
3. In another bowl beat eggs lightly and stir in milk, brandy, lemon juice, lemon rind, and apple.
4. Add egg mixture to fruit mixture and mix well. Turn

into greased bowl. Cover bowl with circle of waxed paper and then with aluminum foil. Secure with string.

5. Place bowl in 7- to 8-quart casserole and add sufficient boiling water to come halfway up sides of bowl. Cover casserole and steam over low heat for 6 hours, adding more boiling water as needed.

6. Unmold pudding and flame. Serve with hard sauce. Puddings may be made 6 to 8 weeks before the holiday season. Store in a cool place, then before serving, steam for 1½ hours.

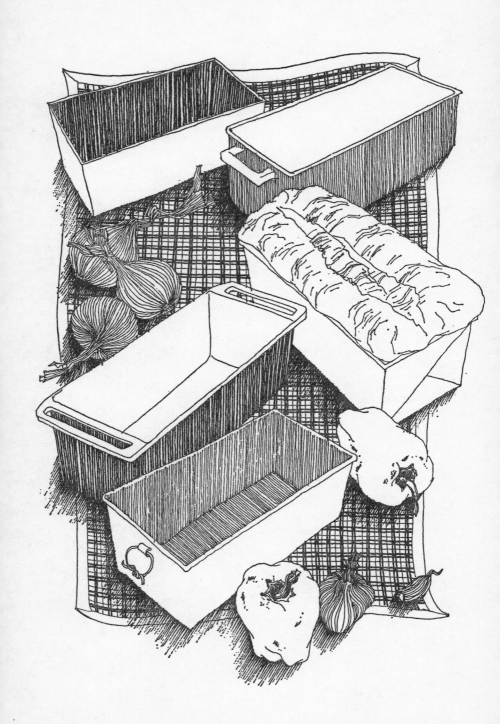

6

THE LOAF PAN

A loaf pan is a deep rectangular pan with slightly flaring sides, made of ovenware glass, aluminum, or other metals, used primarily for baking bread, for fish, meat, or vegetable loaves and for loaf cakes. It is by no means essential, but is relatively inexpensive and nice to have to add another dimension to your cookware and your cooking.

There are many different sizes of loaf pans, but the best all-purpose size is one called 9-inch that actually measures $8\frac{1}{2} \times 4\frac{1}{2} \times 2\frac{3}{4}$. This has a liquid capacity of $1\frac{1}{2}$ quarts, which is the same capacity as your small open baker. So, if you don't have a loaf pan and wish to make any of the recipes in this chapter you may substitute your $10 \times 6 \times 2$-inch baker. The oven time for meat loaves and cakes baked in the open baker instead of the loaf pan will be from 10 to 15 minutes less, since there is a greater surface area exposed to the oven heat. Anytime you change a receptacle from the one specified in the recipe to another, you will have to watch your cooking time. When a meat loaf begins to shrink from the edge of the pan, and when a cake tester inserted in the center of a cake comes out clean, these foods are ready to take from the oven.

ALL-BEEF GLAZED MEAT LOAF
Serves 8

2½ pounds ground lean
  beef
1 cup milk
2 cups soft bread
  crumbs
2½ teaspoons salt
¼ teaspoon pepper
½ cup shredded raw
  carrots

½ cup minced onion
2 eggs, lightly beaten
½ cup catsup
3 tablespoons brown
  sugar
1 tablespoon prepared
  mustard

1. Preheat oven to 325° F.
2. In mixing bowl mix thoroughly the beef, milk, bread crumbs, salt, pepper, carrots, onion, and eggs.
3. Pack meat mixture firmly into 9-inch loaf pan.
4. Combine catsup, brown sugar, and mustard. Spread over top of meat loaf.
5. Bake in preheated oven for 1½ hours.

SAVORY MEAT LOAF
Serves 8

2 cups fresh bread
crumbs
8-ounce can tomato
sauce
1 pound ground beef
½ pound ground veal
½ pound ground pork
¼ cup chopped parsley
¾ cup finely chopped
onion
½ cup finely chopped
green pepper

2 eggs, lightly beaten
2 teaspoons salt
¼ teaspoon pepper
2 teaspoons
Worcestershire sauce
½ teaspoon sugar
½ teaspoon dried basil
or tarragon
1 cup shredded Cheddar
cheese

1. Preheat oven to 350° F. Grease 9-inch loaf pan.
2. In mixing bowl combine crumbs and tomato sauce.
Add remaining ingredients and mix well.
3. Turn mixture into loaf pan and bake in preheated
oven for 1½ hours.
4. Let stand for 5 minutes, then drain off excess liquid.
Turn out onto serving dish and serve with flavorful tomato sauce.

DEVILED HAM LOAF
Serves 6

1½ cups cooked ham
1 medium onion,
   quartered
1 stalk celery, quartered
10 slices bread
½ cup parsley sprigs

3 eggs
2 teaspoons
   Worcestershire sauce
2 teaspoons prepared
   mustard
¼ teaspoon pepper

1. Put ham, onion, celery, bread, and parsley through medium blade of meat grinder.
2. Preheat oven to 350° F. Line bottom of a 9-inch loaf pan with wax paper and grease paper.
3. Combine eggs with Worcestershire, mustard, and pepper. Mix with ham mixture. Turn into prepared pan.
4. Bake in preheated oven for 1 hour and 15 minutes.
5. Cool loaf for 5 minutes, then unmold onto serving dish. Remove wax paper and serve hot.

SALMON RICE LOAF
Serves 6

¼ cup dry bread
   crumbs
1-pound can salmon
2 cups cooked rice
3 eggs, beaten
½ cup chopped green
   onions
¼ cup finely chopped
   green pepper

¼ cup chopped parsley
1 tablespoon capers
   with liquid
⅛ teaspoon Tabasco
2 teaspoons lemon juice
½ teaspoon salt
⅛ teaspoon pepper

1. Preheat oven to 350° F. Line 9-inch loaf pan with alumimum foil and grease well. Press crumbs onto bottom and sides of pan.
2. Drain salmon, reserving liquid. Bone and remove skin from salmon.
3. Flake salmon and add all remaining ingredients. Mix well. Turn into prepared pan.
4. Bake in preheated oven for 1 hour. Remove from oven, let stand 5 minutes, then unmold onto serving dish. Remove foil and serve hot.

MIXED VEGETABLE LOAF
Serves 6

¼ cup dry bread crumbs
¼ cup butter or
    margarine
1 large onion, chopped
¼ cup chopped green
    pepper
1 cup chopped celery
1 cup chopped
    mushrooms

¼ cup flour
¼ cup milk
2 eggs, beaten
2 cups grated carrots
1½ cups cooked peas
1 teaspoon salt
⅛ teaspoon pepper
Dash Tabasco

1. Preheat oven to 350° F. Line 9-inch loaf pan with aluminum foil. Grease foil well and coat with crumbs.
2. In 10-inch skillet melt butter or margarine, and in it sauté onion, green pepper, and celery for 5 minutes. Add mushrooms, and sauté for 2 minutes longer.
3. Sprinkle vegetables with flour and gradually stir in milk. Cook, stirring constantly, until sauce is thick.
4. Remove from heat and stir in eggs, carrots, peas, salt, pepper, and Tabasco.

5. Turn into prepared pan and bake in preheated oven for 1 hour, or until center is firm.
6. Remove from oven, let stand for 5 minutes, then unmold onto serving dish. Discard foil and serve with egg sauce (see Index).

VEAL AND HAM PIE
Serves 8

1 pound cooked ham
1 large onion
1 stalk celery
2½ pounds ground veal
2 cups fresh bread
    crumbs
1 teaspoon salt
¼ teaspoon pepper
2 teaspoons
    Worcestershire sauce
2 tablespoons chopped
    parsley

¼ teaspoon dried
    tarragon
Pastry for a 2-crust pie
3 hard-cooked eggs
1 egg yolk
1 tablespoon milk
10½-ounce can beef
    consommé with
    gelatin

1. Put ham, onion, and celery through medium blade of meat grinder. Mix with veal, crumbs, salt, pepper, Worcestershire sauce, parsley, and tarragon.
2. Preheat oven to 450° F. Grease 9-inch loaf pan.
3. Roll out ¾ of the pastry ⅛ inch thick into a large rectangle. Line sides and bottom of prepared pan, allowing excess pastry to hang over top.
4. Press half the meat mixture into lined pan. Place eggs in a row on top and top with remaining meat mixture.
5. Roll out remaining pastry ⅛ inch thick. Place on top

of meat and seal wedges together well. Make a hole in center of pastry.

6. Arrange pastry "leaves" around hole in pastry. Brush pastry with egg yolk lightly beaten with milk.

7. Bake in preheated oven for 10 minutes. Reduce oven temperature to 350° F. and continue to bake for 1½ hours longer. Cover pie lightly with aluminum foil if pastry begins to get too brown.

8. Cool pie in the pan, then unmold onto serving dish. Turn right side up.

9. Meanwhile boil consommé until reduced to about ½ cup. Cool slightly, then pour through the hole in the pastry, using a small funnel or meat baster. Chill until serving time.

COLE SLAW MOLD
Serves 8

*6-ounce package
lemon-flavored gelatin
1 cup boiling water
½ cup cider vinegar
1 cup cold water
1 cup mayonnaise
2 teaspoons
Worcestershire sauce
1 tablespoon prepared
mustard*

*Salt and pepper to taste
1 medium onion, grated
4 cups shredded cabbage
2 carrots, shredded
½ cup chopped green
pepper
½ cup chopped radishes*

1. Oil 9-inch loaf pan lightly.

2. Dissolve gelatin in boiling water, and stir in vinegar, cold water, mayonnaise, Worcestershire, and mustard. Stir

until smooth. Season with salt and pepper, and chill until mixture begins to thicken.

3. Fold in all vegetables. Turn mixture into loaf pan and chill until firm.

4. Unmold onto cold serving dish and garnish with salad greens.

CHICKEN IN ASPIC
Serves 6

2 envelopes plain gelatin
3½ cups chicken stock
  or broth
1 egg white and crushed
  shell
1 hard-cooked egg,
  sliced
Thin slivers of ripe olive
1 teaspoon Worcestershire
  sauce
⅛ teaspoon Tabasco
Salt and pepper

3 cups diced cooked
  chicken
1 medium green pepper,
  finely diced
1 small onion, grated
1 cup finely chopped
  celery
1 cup finely chopped
  parsley
¼ cup chopped canned
  pimientos

1. Oil 9-inch loaf pan.

2. In a 2½-quart saucepan soften gelatin in ½ cup chicken stock. Add remaining chicken stock, egg white and shell, and heat over medium heat, whisking constantly, until mixture boils up once in pan. Remove from heat and allow to settle. Carefully pour liquid through a strainer lined with a kitchen towel. The resulting aspic will be crystal clear.

3. Pour ½ cup of the aspic into prepared pan and chill until set.

4. Arrange egg slices and olive slivers in bottom of pan to form a decorative design. Add another ½ cup aspic and chill until set.

5. Stir into remaining aspic the Worcestershire, Tabasco, salt and pepper to season mixture well, chicken, green pepper, onion, celery, parsley and pimientos. Chill until mixture begins to thicken.

6. Spoon mixture into prepared pan and chill until firm. Unmold onto serving dish and garnish with lettuce greens.

AVOCADO CHICKEN MOLD

Serves 8

2 envelopes plain gelatin	Salt and pepper to taste
3 cups chicken broth	2½ cups diced cooked
2 avocados	chicken
1 cup commercial sour	1 cup chopped celery
cream	⅓ cup chopped green
2 teaspoons	pepper
Worcestershire sauce	¼ cup chopped canned
Few dashes Tabasco	pimientos
1 small onion, grated	

1. Oil a 9-inch loaf pan lightly.

2. Soften gelatin in ½ cup chicken broth in saucepan. Add 1 cup chicken broth and cook over low heat, stirring constantly, until gelatin is thoroughly dissolved. Pour into mixing bowl, and stir in remaining broth.

3. Peel avocados and discard seeds. Mash avocados in a small bowl and blend well with the sour cream.

4. Add avocado mixture, Worcestershire, Tabasco, and onion to gelatin mixture, and beat until smooth. Season

with salt and pepper, and chill until mixture begins to thicken.

5. Stir in chicken, celery, green pepper, and pimientos, and turn into loaf pan.

6. Chill until firm. Unmold onto cold serving dish and surround by crisp salad greens.

CHEESE CHIVE BREAD
Makes 1 loaf

1 envelope active dry yeast
½ cup lukewarm water
2½ cups all-purpose flour
1 teaspoon sugar
1 teaspoon salt
¼ teaspoon dry mustard
Dash cayenne

2 tablespoons chopped chives or green onion tops
½ cup lukewarm milk
1 tablespoon oil
1 egg
1 cup shredded sharp Cheddar cheese

1. Grease 9-inch loaf pan.
2. Dissolve yeast in warm water.
3. Into mixing bowl sift flour, sugar, salt, mustard, and cayenne. Stir in chives. Make a well in center of flour mixture and pour yeast mixture into it. Add milk, oil, and egg. Beat with the hand until mixture leaves sides of bowl. Turn out of bowl onto floured surface and knead until dough is smooth, adding cheese gradually as you knead.
4. Shape into loaf and set into loaf pan. Cover and let rise for about 2 hours, or until double in bulk.

5. Meanwhile preheat oven to 350° F.
6. Bake loaf in preheated oven for 55 minutes. Turn out onto wire rack to cool.

RAISIN BREAKFAST BREAD
Makes 9-inch loaf

2 cups all-purpose flour
2 teaspoons baking powder
¼ teaspoon salt
1 teaspoon cinnamon
⅓ cup shortening
¾ cup firmly packed brown sugar

¾ cup milk
1 egg
½ teaspoon almond extract
1 cup seedless raisins
½ cup chopped blanched almonds

1. Preheat oven to 350° F. Grease 9-inch loaf pan.
2. In mixing bowl combine flour, baking powder, salt, and cinnamon.
3. Cut in shortening with pastry cutter or two knives until mixture looks like bread crumbs. Stir in sugar.
4. Combine milk, egg, and almond extract. Add to flour, and stir just to moisten all dry ingredients.
5. Stir in raisins and almonds and turn batter into prepared pan.
6. Bake in preheated oven for 55 minutes, or until bread tests done with a wooden pick.
7. Turn out of pan onto wire rack to cool.

RASPBERRY CHARLOTTE RUSSE

Serves 8

3-ounce package lady
  fingers, split lengthwise
1-pound package frozen
  raspberries, thawed
1 envelope plain gelatin

3 egg yolks
¾ cup sugar
1 cup heavy cream,
  whipped

1.   Line bottom of 9-inch loaf pan with wax paper. Butter sides and bottom of pan. Line bottom and sides with lady fingers.
2.   Force raspberries with liquid through sieve or purée in an electric blender and strain to remove seeds.
3.   Soften gelatin in ½ cup of the raspberry purée. Stir over simmering water until gelatin is thoroughly dissolved. Stir dissolved gelatin into remaining purée, and cool.
4.   Put egg yolks and sugar in saucepan, and beat over simmering water until sugar granules have dissolved.
5.   Blend egg-yolk mixture into raspberry purée, and cool until mixture begins to set.
6.   Fold in whipped cream and spoon into prepared pan.
7.   Chill until filling is firm.
8.   Trim excess edges of lady fingers around top of pan and place on top of filling. Unmold onto serving dish and decorate with additional whipped cream if desired.

RUM BUMBLE
Serves 6

1 *envelope plain gelatin*
⅓ *cup water*
½ *cup sugar*
2 *tablespoons rum*
¼ *cup scotch*

2 *egg whites*
1 *cup heavy cream,*
  whipped
½ *cup chopped toasted*
  almonds

1. Oil 9-inch loaf pan lightly.
2. Soften gelatin in water in cup or small bowl. Set into a skillet containing a little hot water and cook over low heat, stirring occasionally, until gelatin is thoroughly dissolved.
3. Turn gelatin into a mixing bowl, and stir in sugar, rum, and scotch. Chill until mixture begins to thicken. Then beat until foamy.
4. In another mixing bowl beat egg whites until stiff, but not dry. Gradually add beaten egg whites to gelatin mixture and continue to beat until mixture is smooth and glossy.
5. Fold in whipped cream and turn into loaf pan. Chill until firm.
6. Unmold on serving dish and sprinkle with almonds.

MELON-BALL MOLD
Serves 6

*1-pound package frozen
    melon balls, thawed*
*6-ounce package
    lemon-flavored gelatin*
Water
*6-ounce package cream
    cheese*

*1 teaspoon grated lemon
    rind*
1 egg white
¼ cup sugar

1.   Oil a 9-inch loaf pan lightly. Drain melon balls and reserve liquid.
2.   Dissolve gelatin in 1 cup boiling water. Add reserved melon liquid and sufficient water to make a total of 3 cups liquid.
3.   Pour 1 cup gelatin into loaf pan, and chill until set.
4.   Arrange melon balls in pan and add another cup gelatin. Chill until set.
5.   Beat cream cheese until light and fluffy. Gradually beat in remaining cup gelatin and lemon rind. Chill until mixture begins to thicken.
6.   Beat egg white until foamy. Gradually beat in sugar, and continue to beat until meringue is stiff and glossy. Fold into cream-cheese mixture and spoon into loaf pan. Chill until firm.
7.   Unmold on chilled serving dish and keep cold until serving time.

MELON MOUSSE
Serves 8

1 ripe cantaloupe
Water
1 envelope plain gelatin
3-ounce package
  lemon-flavored gelatin

½ cup sugar
1 cup heavy cream,
  whipped

1. Oil a 9-inch loaf pan lightly.
2. Cut melon in half and discard seeds. Scoop out flesh of melon and press through a sieve or food mill or purée in an electric blender.
3. In 2- or 2½-quart saucepan mix plain gelatin with lemon gelatin and sugar. Stir in ½ cup water. Cook over low heat, stirring constantly, until gelatin is thoroughly dissolved.
4. Mix gelatin with melon purée and chill until mixture begins to thicken.
5. Fold in whipped cream and spoon into loaf pan. Chill until set.
6. Unmold onto serving dish and surround by additional melon balls or garnish with whipped cream, as desired.

RAINBOW LOAF
Serves 8

3-ounce package
orange-flavored gelatin
Boiling water
2 medium oranges peeled
and finely diced
3-ounce package
strawberry-flavored
gelatin

½ cup commercial sour
cream
3-ounce package
lemon-flavored gelatin

1. Oil a 9-inch loaf pan lightly.
2. Dissolve orange gelatin in 1 cup boiling water. Stir in ½ cup cold water and the oranges. Pour into loaf pan and chill until set.
3. Dissolve strawberry gelatin in 1 cup boiling water. Stir in ¾ cup cold water and the sour cream. Beat until smooth. Pour strawberry mixture over orange gelatin and chill until set.
4. Dissolve lemon gelatin in 1 cup boiling water. Stir in ¾ cup cold water. Pour into mold over strawberry mixture and chill until firm.
5. When ready to serve, unmold and decorate with fruit or with whipped cream as desired.

CHOCOLATE MOUSSE LOAF

Serves 8

1 envelope plain gelatin
2 cups milk
¾ cup sugar
3 ounces (3 squares)
  unsweetened
  chocolate, shredded

3 egg yolks, beaten
1 teaspoon rum flavoring
3 egg whites, stiffly
  beaten
1 cup heavy cream,
  whipped

1. Oil a 9-inch loaf pan lightly.
2. In a 2-quart saucepan combine gelatin and milk. Stir in sugar and add chocolate. Cook over low heat, stirring constantly, until mixture is hot and chocolate is melted.
3. Remove from stove and stir in egg yolks and rum flavoring. Cool, stirring occasionally, until mixture begins to thicken and mounds when dropped from spoon.
4. Fold in beaten egg whites and whipped cream. Turn into loaf pan and chill until set.
5. Unmold onto chilled serving plate and, if desired, garnish with additional whipped cream.

VELVET CREAM
Serves 8

2 envelopes plain gelatin
½ cup cold water
2 egg yolks
⅓ cup sugar
Dash salt

1 teaspoon vanilla
1 cup milk
½ cup sweet sherry
2 cups heavy cream,
    whipped

1.   Oil 9-inch loaf pan lightly.
2.   In small bowl or cup soften gelatin in water. Place bowl or cup in skillet of hot water, and cook over low heat until gelatin is dissolved.
3.   In mixing bowl beat egg yolks with sugar until mixture is thick and pale in color. Stir in salt, vanilla, milk, sherry, and gelatin. Cool until mixture begins to thicken.
4.   Fold in whipped cream and turn into loaf pan. Chill until firm.
5.   Unmold onto cold serving plate and, if desired, surround by fresh or canned fruits.

CREAM OF RICE LOAF
Serves 8

2 envelopes plain gelatin
½ cup cold water
1½ cups milk
1 teaspoon vanilla
3 egg yolks, beaten
½ cup sugar
⅓ cup dark rum
2 cups cooked rice

⅓ cup chopped walnuts
⅓ cup toasted coconut
    flakes
½ cup finely chopped
    mixed candied peel
1 cup heavy cream,
    whipped

1. Oil 9-inch loaf pan lightly.
2. In cup or small bowl soften gelatin in cold water. Set in skillet of hot water and cook over low heat until gelatin is dissolved.
3. In 2-quart saucepan combine milk, vanilla, egg yolks, and sugar. Cook over moderate heat, stirring vigorously, until mixture just coats the spoon. Do not let mixture boil. When bubbles begin to appear around edge of saucepan, remove pan from heat and continue to stir briskly.
4. Stir in dissolved gelatin and rum. Let cool, stirring occasionally, until mixture starts to thicken.
5. Stir in rice, walnuts, coconut flakes, and candied peel. Fold in whipped cream.
6. Turn into loaf pan and chill until set.
7. Unmold on cold serving plate and decorate with candied cherries.

PINEAPPLE-ORANGE CREAM LOAF
Serves 8

6-ounce package
orange-flavored gelatin
1 cup boiling water
1-pound 4-ounce can
crushed pineapple
Cold water

½ cup orange juice
3-ounce package lady
fingers
1 cup heavy cream,
whipped

1. Oil a 9-inch loaf pan lightly.
2. Dissolve gelatin in boiling water.
3. Drain pineapple into a large measuring cup and add sufficient cold water to make a total of 2 cups liquid. Stir into gelatin mixture.

4. Mix 1 cup gelatin mixture with the crushed pineapple and set aside.

5. Add orange juice to remaining gelatin mixture.

6. Pour about ½ cup gelatin into loaf pan and chill until set. Split lady fingers and arrange half, top side down, in pan. Pour about 1 cup gelatin into pan over lady fingers and chill until set.

7. Fold whipped cream into pineapple mixture and spread in loaf pan. Chill until set.

8. Arrange remaining lady fingers, top side up, on pineapple mixture and add remaining gelatin. Chill until set.

9. Unmold onto chilled serving dish and decorate with additional whipped cream if desired.

SIMPLE SIMON CHEESE CAKE
Serves 6

1 cup graham cracker crumbs	2 8-ounce packages cream cheese
½ cup plus 2 tablespoons sugar	2 eggs
⅓ cup melted butter	1 teaspoon vanilla
	Dash salt

1. Grease 9-inch loaf pan. Preheat oven to 350° F.

2. Prepare crumb crust: Combine crumbs with 2 tablespoons sugar. Stir in melted butter and mix well. Press mixture onto bottom and halfway up sides of prepared pan.

3. Prepare cheese filling: In mixing bowl beat cream cheese until soft and smooth. Beat in remaining ½ cup sugar, eggs, vanilla, and salt, and beat until smooth and creamy.

4. Pour filling into lined pan and bake in preheated oven for 45 minutes.

5. Cool, then chill until serving time. Unmold onto serving dish.

DELUXE COFFEECAKE

Makes 1 loaf

1 *pound loaf uncooked frozen bread, thawed*
½ *cup melted butter or margarine*
¾ *cup firmly packed brown sugar*

1 *teaspoon cinnamon*
¾ *cup chopped walnuts*
½ *cup chopped glacé cherries*

1. Preheat oven to 375° F. Grease 9-inch loaf pan.

2. Cut thawed dough into pieces the size of walnuts and roll each into a ball.

3. Dip balls into melted butter or margarine and roll in sugar mixed with cinnamon.

4. Arrange about half the balls in prepared pan and sprinkle with half the nuts and cherries. Repeat layers until all balls of dough, nuts, and cherries have been used. Sprinkle with remaining sugar and melted butter.

5. Cover and let rise for about 1 hour, or until dough is doubled in bulk.

6. Bake in preheated oven for 40 minutes.

7. Turn out on wire rack to cool. Enjoy warm or cold.

ORANGE COCONUT CAKE
Makes 1 loaf

2 cups cake flour
2 teaspoons baking
  powder
Dash salt
¾ cup butter
¾ cup sugar

3 eggs
¼ cup orange juice
1½ tablespoons grated
  orange rind
1 cup flaked toasted
  coconut

1. Preheat oven to 350° F. Grease a 9-inch loaf pan.
2. Sift together flour, baking powder, and salt onto piece of wax paper.
3. In mixing bowl cream butter and sugar until light and fluffy. Add eggs, one at a time, alternately with flour mixture and orange juice, beating well after each addition.
4. Stir in orange rind and coconut.
5. Turn batter into loaf pan and bake in preheated oven for 1 hour, or until cake tests done.
6. Cool for 5 minutes, then turn cake out of pan to cool on wire cake rack.

OLD-FASHIONED POUND CAKE
Makes 1 loaf

1 cup butter
1¼ cups sugar
1 teaspoon vanilla
1 teaspoon grated orange
  rind
4 eggs

2 cups sifted cake flour
½ teaspoon salt
1 teaspoon double-acting
  baking powder
¼ teaspoon mace
¼ cup milk

1. Preheat oven to 325° F. Oil a 9-inch loaf pan.
2. In mixing bowl cream together butter, sugar, vanilla, and orange rind until mixture is light and fluffy.
3. Add eggs, one at a time, beating well after each addition.
4. Combine flour, salt, baking powder, and mace.
5. Stir flour mixture into butter mixture alternately with the milk.
6. Pour batter into loaf pan and bake in preheated oven for 1¼ to 1½ hours, or until cake tester comes out clean.
7. Let cool for 5 minutes, then turn out on wire cake rack to cool completely.

CHRISTMAS FRUIT CAKE
Makes 2¾-pound loaf

½ cup halved glacé cherries (3½-ounce jar)
½ cup chopped walnuts
¾ cup chopped candied lemon peel (4-ounce jar)
¾ cup currants
1 cup seedless raisins
¾ cup seedless golden raisins
1½ cups all-purpose flour

¼ teaspoon each salt, nutmeg, cinnamon, mace, and ginger
1 teaspoon baking powder
½ cup butter
¾ cup firmly packed brown sugar
3 eggs
¼ cup brandy

1. Line sides and bottom of 9-inch loaf pan with double layer of wax paper. Grease side of paper next to pan. Wrap

outside of pan with brown paper and secure with string. Wax paper and brown paper should extend about 1 inch above edge of pan. Place pan on baking sheet.

2. Preheat oven to 275° F.

3. In large mixing bowl combine cherries, walnuts, lemon peel, currants, raisins with ½ cup of the flour.

4. Sift onto square of wax paper the remaining flour with salt, spices, and baking powder.

5. In another mixing bowl cream butter and sugar together until light and fluffy.

6. Add eggs, one at a time, alternately with sifted flour mixture, beating well after each addition.

7. Add fruit mixture and stir until blended.

8. Turn batter into prepared pan and make a deep well in center of batter.

9. Bake in preheated oven for 3 hours, or until cake tests done with wooden pick.

10. Cool cake in pan on wire rack, then remove from pan and peel off papers.

11. Turn cake upside down and pierce all over with a wooden pick. Sprinkle cake with brandy. Wrap tightly in foil and store in a cool place for 2 to 3 weeks before cutting.

POTS AND PANS INDEX

RECIPE INDEX

EQUIVALENTS

ingredient	quantity	equivalent
bananas	3 medium	1 pound
breadcrumbs	1 cup	2¾ ounces
butter	1 pound	2 cups
	1 stick	½ cup
	4 tablespoons	½ stick
cheese	1 pound	4 cups, grated
chocolate	1 square	1 ounce
cocoanut, shredded	1 pound	5 cups
coffee, ground	1 pound	3½ cups
cornstarch	1 pound	3 cups
cranberries	1 pound	4 cups
cream, heavy	1 cup	2 cups whipped
dates, chopped pitted	1 cup	6 ounces
eggs, whole	1 cup	5
egg yolks	1 cup	approx. 16
egg whites	1 cup	approx. 8
flour, bread, sifted	1 pound	4 cups
flour, cake, sifted	1 pound	4½ cups